PRINTING'S ALIVE

A TALE OF INK, INNOVATION, AND
INDUSTRY WISDOM

Warren Werbitt

quratebooks.com

Book Creation Services

by

It's time you tell your story

www.bookmystorypublishing.com

A venture of

PRINTING'S ALIVE:
A TALE OF INK, INNOVATION, AND INDUSTRY WISDOM
Warren Werbitt

©Warren Werbitt

Published in 2024

© Published by

Qurate Books Pvt. Ltd.
Goa 403523, India
www.quratebooks.com
Tel: 1800-210-6527, Email: info@quratebooks.com

ISBN: 978-93-58983-78-4

Me and the late Peter Rollit, my friend and mentor

Foreword

Warren Werbitt, "The Print Whisperer", is widely recognized within the print industry where he has made significant contributions as an entrepreneur, influencer, and advocate. His journey began with the founding of a print communications company which, under his leadership, flourished into a bustling enterprise boasting 120 employees and an impressive $19 million in annual sales. Werbitt's dynamic approach to business, coupled with his fervent passion for print, a razor-sharp wit, and a refreshingly outspoken demeanor, has not only captured but also held the attention of industry peers and observers alike. His active engagement with industry associations, peer groups, and presence in the media reflect his deep commitment to the printing industry, offering candid insights into its future prospects and inherent challenges.t6

My introduction to Warren came through a serendipitous encounter with his 2008 YouTube sensation, "Printing's Alive," where his animated rant on the vitality of print, as the founder of Pazazz Printing, immediately resonated with me. The video's humor and passion prompted me to reach out for permission to feature it on WhatTheyThink.com, where it continues to be a topic of conversation. This initial interaction not only marked the beginning of a professional connection but also kindled a friendship anchored in mutual respect, a shared commitment to uplift others, and a collective love for the printing industry. Our bond has been a constant through various professional and personal trials, underscoring the invaluable nature of such camaraderie. You cannot overvalue such a thing.

My foray into the printing world was somewhat unconventional, transitioning from a career in the automotive industry, where I specialized in the technical cleaning of paint shops and dirt in paint analysis, to joining WhatTheyThink in 2002. The familiar scent of printing inks, reminiscent of automotive paints, made me feel instantly at home in a print shop. By the time Werbitt's video went viral in 2008, our team was already deep into video content development, but his unique persona was unlike anything we had encountered. Today, he hosts the very popular "Printer to Printer" podcast on WhatTheyThink. com and Spotify, where his real-world experience and candid approach resonate deeply with our audience.

I see reflections of my own journey in Warren's path - from early entrepreneurial experiments and setbacks to continual reinvention and adaptation. I relate to the grassroots efforts of Warren and his brother licking envelopes in the early days, reminiscent of me early on at WhatTheyThink, scouring the internet into the early hours to find enough news stories to curate for our newsletter. We weren't always overrun with press releases back in the early days!

I've also always related to Warren's "work hard, play hard" nature as that has been a core part of the WhatTheyThink ethos from day one. I've literally been out drinking with this guy all over the world - from Prague to Portland and back again. He, like me, knows that many of the best ideas happen over happy hour - or, in our case, much later!

One of the most compelling aspects of Werbitt's narrative is his adept navigation through industry upheavals and his embrace of change. This is particularly evident in the chapter "Navigating Industry Storms and Embracing Change," where he offers an overview of the many ways the industry has changed over the years and how he has addressed that change through innovation and creative approaches to problems. Sometimes even skirting the lines of "corporate espionage". I've found in my business career this can be the area where many struggle. The unexpected economic downturn. That one big account we didn't expect to lose. The out-of-left field global pandemic. Add to that the sometimes subtle nature of change within industries - those slight shifts that can sometimes be imperceptible until we find ourselves rearranging the proverbial deck chairs on the Titanic. These can be the most challenging times requiring the best of what an entrepreneur and business person has to offer. Warren offers some real-world actionable insights in how to handle these types of situations that will be of value to anyone in business, but especially those in the printing industry.

If you are interested in understanding the printing industry's future or seeking wisdom peppered with remarkable and often amusing anecdotes, Werbitt's book is a treasure trove. His character, marked by a blend of expertise, resilience, and a knack for storytelling, serves as a rich source of inspiration and guidance.

Warren's contributions to the printing industry are marked by his enthusiasm, expertise, and a genuine desire to see the industry thrive, making him a respected and influential figure among his peers and colleagues. This book is another step in that direction and will be a valuable resource for those wanting to improve their print businesses or just wanted to gain some insights from a battle-tested entrepreneur.

In my reading, I have been keenly aware of the potential telling of any stories related to me and to my relief found none. Some stories are best left for the bar. Ask us sometime. We'll tell you.

Eric Vessels

President, WhatTheyThink

At the Graph Expo 2017

Preface

You know, they say a picture is worth a thousand words, but if I had to translate my thoughts into print, I'd need a whole library of encyclopaedias! I've always been more of a chatterbox than a scribbler, but today, I'm breaking out the spine, well, metaphorically at least.

Why? Because I'm about to share what's near and dear to my heart – the print industry. An industry that represents more than ink on paper, it embodies a world of creativity, innovation, and endless possibilities. I've poured my soul into these pages because rather than just read this book once and toss it aside,

I want you to hold it close, like an old friend, to dog-ear the pages, and refer to it often.

Now you might wonder, why should I care about some print industry introspection? Well, let me tell you, I've been through the ups, the downs, and the loop-de-loops of this industry. I've stumbled, I've soared, and I've even face-planted a few times. But through it all, I've learned some valuable lessons.

I don't want you to make the same mistakes I did. I want you to learn from my experiences because, trust me, you're going to want to know. I've seen it all – the good, the bad, and the "what was I thinking?" moments. You see, this book isn't just a collection of words; it's an extension of me, my passion, my blood, sweat, and more than a few tears.

Imagine a world where you can avoid the pitfalls I stumbled into, where you can sidestep those awkward moments, or how to pick the right people to surround yourself with. Picture yourself running your print business with unbridled zeal and entrepreneurial fire. That's the goal I want you to benefit from the most. Your success is my success, and that's not just a catchy phrase, it's my mission.

I must tip my hat (or in my case, my ink-stained fingers) to Abe Gonshor, a family friend who ignited my fascination with the print industry. Abe introduced me to the Macintosh

Computer when it was just a baby in the tech world; I instantly understood why Steve Jobs designed it the way he did. It was like magic in a box, a digital canvas that could bring ideas to life. That Mac revolutionized the print and publishing industry – it was a game-changer. Thank you, Abe, for pushing me in that direction; you're a true print wizard.

I vividly remember the day Abe shared the Mac's wonders with me. I dashed out and bought not one, but two of those miracle machines for my business. And you know what? They were just the beginning. I made a series of bold moves – from investing in cutting-edge print machines to outsmarting the competition with my Macs.

This book isn't just for seasoned industry veterans; it's for the newcomers, the rookies eager to make their mark. In this digital age, where everything seems to be at the touch of a screen, print still stands tall. It's not just surviving; it's thriving, evolving, and adapting to new technologies. As a print enthusiast, I've witnessed these technological changes firsthand.

Print is a visual delight that can mesmerize anyone with its results. The technology and machines we use today bring life to concepts and creative artworks. It's not just a solitary industry but a vibrant ecosystem that includes graphic design, paper, information technology, logistics, shipping, events, and advertising. Print is everywhere, and the potential is immense.

You see, print touches every aspect of our lives. From the morning newspaper that fuels your day to the packaging of your favourite snacks, from the posters that inspire you to the magazines that entertain you – print is all around us, painting the world with colours and ideas.

So, I leave you with this – a vision of a thriving industry where your passion, your dreams, and your dedication can make a difference. Let this book be your guiding star as you navigate the exciting, ever-evolving world of print. Together, we can paint a future that's brighter, more colourful, and filled with endless possibilities. I'm here to inspire, to guide, and to share, because I love print.

Acknowledgment

In the spectrum of life, some threads shimmer brighter, weaving through the fabric of our existence with such vibrancy that they colour our very being. As I stand at the threshold of a new chapter, my heart brims with gratitude for the constellation of souls who've illuminated my path.

To the late Peter Rollit, whose spirit dances in the margins of every page I write. Peter was more than a friend; he was a print partner, an inspiration, and a mentor whose wisdom echoes in my thoughts daily. His legacy is like a lighthouse that guides me, a reminder of the strength found in kindness and collaboration.

Abe Gonshor, a family friend with a compass heart, he steered me towards "the Mac," and set me on a course that has led to shores I never dreamed I could reach. Abe, your direction was the nudge I needed to embark on this journey, and for that, I am eternally grateful.

The late Aaron Fish, founder of Ilco Unican, a visionary who taught me to see the soul of the world through the lens of humanity. Aaron, your offering was not just advice but a transformational shift in perspective, allowing me to embrace the richness of human connection.

Jonathan Weiner, the silent force of nature. Jonathan, your leadership in both community and business serves as a lighthouse for many, myself included. You've shown me the power of moving forward, even when the path is unseen, and the importance of leaving footprints for others to follow.

Joanne Gore, the bridge between worlds, thank you for your guidance, for connecting dots in a constellation I couldn't see, and for having me introduced to Rajnish Shirsat, who has helped me become an Author. Our friendship is a treasure, a testament to the journey we've embarked upon together, navigating the seas of creativity and collaboration.

Shawn Werbitt, not just my brother but my business partner. Our shared dreams and challenges have woven us closer, creating a bond that transcends the mere familial. Together, we've built more than a business; we've crafted a legacy.

Andrew Small, my brother in blood and in the branding world. Your creativity has given voice to my vision, dressing it in a suit of elegance and impact. You are the artist of my thoughts, the designer of dreams.

Eric Vessels, a friend not confined by geography but connected through countless shared experiences across the globe. Our journeys have been punctuated by laughter, learning, and the occasional libation, making the world feel a little smaller, but a lot friendlier.

Harold Simpkin, whose university class was an oasis in a desert of academia. Your teachings resonated with me, sparking a curiosity that has fueled my endeavours. And to James, your son, my steadfast fishing buddy—our escapades are the threads of joy woven through the fabric of life.

To all of you, and to those whose names are etched in the quiet corners of my heart, thank you. This book is not just a collection of pages but a mosaic of your influence, a testament to the beauty of collective journeying. As these words find their way into the world, know that they carry a piece of each of you, an homage to the light you've gifted me.

Contents

My Journey So Far

School isn't for everybody. It sure wasn't for me. The only class I actually enjoyed was marketing – partially because of my professor, Harold Simpkins – but mainly because it related to the things I saw and touched everyday.

Aside from that, I never resonated with school. In fact, while writing final exams in my second year, I stood up 20 minutes into the process and walked out. I could feel the sudden shock in the room, with professors and proctors looking at me sideways. At that moment, I vowed to be done with school and never look back.

After leaving school, I found myself in the world of fabrics. I was working at my friend's dad's fabric business, selling textiles from one end of the country to the other. My trusty suitcase was jam-packed with samples that we shipped to every fabric store imaginable across Canada. Not the most glamorous gig, but I wore that fabric peddler hat for a solid two years.

Eventually, I was headhunted for another job within the textile industry, but this time, I'd be repping high-end, expensive fabrics. I thought I'd hit the jackpot! Four months into my new gig, the guy who hired me had to let me go. Why? Because he hired me without his partner's consent. I unintentionally became the fall guy in their indecisiveness - and got the boot. But that wasn't the end of my story.

I decided to take matters into my own hands and sued them for wrongful dismissal. Our little legal skirmish ended with a settlement that left me feeling like I'd won the lottery. Ultimately, it funded the engagement ring I used to propose to my future wife. While you could say it was a rocky start, it all worked out in the end.

A few years passed, and I had my fair share of stints here and there. One day, as I was attempting to connect dots that seemed to have no interest in forming a picture, my dad (who owned a print shop) looked at me and quipped, "Why don't you get off your lazy ass and do something?" It was at that moment that I decided to dive headfirst into the world of print.

The genesis of my print journey was a mix of family, a little nudge, and a dash of inspiration. I started visiting my dad's print shop regularly and fell head-over-heels for the world of print. It was like discovering a hidden treasure chest in my own backyard.

Not so long after, I realized I wanted to be my own boss. Luckily, my brother, Shawn, shared this sentiment, so we decided to partner up and set out on our own adventure. We rented a place, owned by an elderly gentleman running a packaging business, got our hands on a few machines and voilà, Pazazz Printing was born. Why Pazazz, you ask? Well, it means "an attractive combination of vitality and glamour," and that's exactly what we wanted our print venture to be.

As time rolled on, we received notice to vacate the rented place, so we packed our bags (and machines) and moved to a new rental, a whopping 2,800 square foot printing playground. Our arsenal included two AB Dick 360 machines and a Hamada 880 two-colour with a single blanket. Our team also started to grow, and we were all buzzing with excitement, living those unforgettable moments of success and firsts. It was the stuff that print dreams are made of.

I was infatuated with the world of print! The intoxicating aroma of paper and board, the inks swirling like a mad scientist's concoction, and the sheer visual ecstasy each project served up. It was like being in a sensory wonderland, and I was Alice, tumbling down the rabbit hole of the printing world.

As a marketing enthusiast, I stumbled upon a revelation that made my heart race with excitement. It was the revelation that every single person I encountered had the potential to become a Pazzaz customer. You see, print isn't just for the bigwigs – it's for everyone, from the person in need of snazzy business cards to the bustling packaging company yearning for that perfect label.

We embraced this concept and started attracting some business. In fact, I have a great story about our very first direct mail project. It was a smaller job of about 1,500 8.5'x11' pieces folded to fit into standard number 10 envelopes. Sounds like a breeze, right? But no one handed us the "envelope playbook", so we were left to our own devices. Now, here's where things took a hilarious turn. While most sane folks would have used a sponge and water to moisten the envelopes, I licked them. Yes, you read that correctly. I licked all 1,500 envelopes like an overzealous postal worker.

By the time I had finished, my tongue had lost all sense of taste and resembled a balloon that had been through a wild party.

But you know what? It was a masterclass in the art of learning from one's mistakes. And if there's one lesson I'll never forget, it's this: in the world of print, sometimes you've got to taste the rainbow, even if it leaves you with a swollen tongue and a story to tell for a lifetime!

Back to the main story, a few years pass and Pazzaz is doing well. I decided to go to the holy grail of printing shows: Drupa.

Now, for those unacquainted with the grandeur of Drupa, it's like 15 huge football fields - fifteen colossal halls, each bursting at the seams with machines that could make even ink-stained print veterans giddy with excitement. I mean, we're talking about machines so mammoth that people lined up in queues, praying for their turn to catch a glimpse of these mechanical behemoths.

To save a few bucks, I'd set up camp a couple of hours away from Dusseldorf, a move that allowed me to squeeze in some much-needed shut-eye on the trains after a long day of print exploration. And let me tell you, I was a nomad on a mission. I must've walked what felt like a gazillion miles within those hallowed convention walls.

Mitsubishi, Manroland, KBA and Heidelberg – you name it, they were all there, strutting their stuff like rock stars at a concert. When those colossal machines roared to life, the very ground beneath my feet danced to their rhythm, and it was sweet music to my ears. For five days straight, I was nothing short of a human exclamation mark, shouting, "Oh My God!" at every turn.

I may have gone a tad overboard with my souvenirs, even by the most enthusiastic collector's standards. I boarded my flight back home with an 80-inch map that Manroland had generously bestowed upon me. Crazy, right? But that wasn't the craziest part. On that flight I was quite a nuisance, annoying my fellow passengers. I could practically hear their grumbling, as I maneuvered my massive map and cornucopia of print samples - but hey, who can blame me for wanting to bring the whole world of print home, right?

Once back home, I surveyed my hundred-pound collection of print samples and had a moment of self-reflection. Why on earth had I carted all of this stuff back? In the grand scheme of things, the inconvenience was a small price to pay for the memories and inspiration that Drupa had gifted me.

However, my heart still harbours a little inkling of disappointment that's left a sour note to my story. You see, while most booths embraced me with open arms, Heidelberg's hospitality was as icy as a Siberian winter. I was treated like a forgotten extra in a blockbuster movie, left twiddling my thumbs for hours, praying that someone would acknowledge my presence. In the end, I left that booth with a heavy heart and vowed never to purchase a Heidelberg machine. The sting of rejection lingered long after I'd left the fairgrounds.

In contrast, Mitsubishi's booth were the true printing knights in shining armor, exuding kindness and a total lack of attitude. Those friendly folks made me feel right at home in their printing kingdom, and for that, they forever hold a special place in my heart.

I can't help but draw a parallel between my chilly Heidelberg encounter and the experiences I've heard about from today's younger generation of millennials and GenZ. It's a lesson in empathy, my friends. We must walk in others' shoes, extend a listening ear, and make newcomers feel at ease. Our future depends on it!

Back in the comfort of my home, I sat down with my dad and my brother, bursting with excitement from my Drupa adventure. I couldn't contain my excitement about the future I saw ahead and proposed that we get ourselves a five-colour press, a beast of a machine with a 20 x 29-inch format. The price tag? A cool million. US.

My trusty accountant quickly shot down my dream. He said, "Sorry, boss, but the numbers just don't add up for that one." I listened to his reasoning, let his words hang in the air for a moment, and then delivered a line that would go down in family lore: "I'm okay with that, but you're fired."

It was a bold move, and it sent shockwaves through our small printing kingdom. But you know what they say about fortune favouring the bold.

My 2nd press Mitsubishi, 28 x 40, 6 color with coater

And so, our journey with that magnificent five-colour press marked the dawn of our grand ascent. We began as a mere whisper in the printing world, nestled in a modest 2,800 square feet of space. But our dreams knew no bounds. From there, we expanded to 3,500, then 4,000 square feet, and finally, our crown jewel, an opulent 85,000 square foot factory space. In an industry where real estate is as coveted as gold, it felt as though we were defying the laws of physics themselves.

This saga of ambition and endurance spanned a remarkable 27 years. It was woven with threads of triumphs and challenges, of soaring highs and gut-wrenching lows. Along this arduous path, I brought a partner on board and with bittersweet resolve parted ways with my brother, who ventured into the world of label printing. He ultimately became one of our most valued clients. Our arsenal swelled with a fleet of machines, and the art of key account management became our guiding star. The Pazazz family grew, and our operation thrived, casting a shimmering glow over our industrious efforts.

But as the saying goes, even the most glorious chapters must eventually turn their page. In the tumultuous year of 2008, the morning newspaper shattered our world with the bleak news of Lehman Brothers' bankruptcy. It was a seismic shock that reverberated through every industry. Panic gripped the air, and our once-eager customers were now retreating, demanding a 25% price cut from the year before. Bloodbath was an understatement. The housing market crumbled, and people clung to every penny.

I found myself in the company of giants like General Motors - Canada, who had also fallen to bankruptcy's grip. Overnight, my once-trusty bank, despite extending a million-and-a-half-dollar line of credit, began to behave like a fair-weathered friend. They did come to my aid, but not before placing a relentless monitor over my every financial move, siphoning off a staggering $20,000 each month.

I thought I was losing my mind - 18 years of hard work seemed to be crashing in front me. I lost my grip, and that night drowned my sorrows in a bottle.

The next morning, I called a company-wide meeting. My voice was shaking, heart laid bare.

I shared our grim reality, assuring them that we were in this together, that no one would be asked to leave, but tough decisions lay ahead, including a painful hit on their paycheques. The room fell silent, but I could sense the weight of understanding in their eyes. Then, I reached out to vendors, suppliers of paper and inks, and our cherished customers. I bared our vulnerability, our resolve, and our path forward.

We do just like the sign says.....
Photo taken 2007 outside plant for Video Printing's Alive

In those trying times, the support that enveloped me from all corners was nothing short of miraculous. It was a testament to the power of effective, honest communication – the power of calling a spade a spade. In the depths of adversity, true relationships are forged and tested. I reflected on my humble beginnings, starting with nothing, only to plummet to rock bottom. But I knew there was only one way from here, and that was up. Slowly, we clawed our way back to normalcy, one resilient step at a time, restoring not just our finances, but the trust and faith of our devoted staff and steadfast allies.

Then, in the midst of my tumultuous journey, there came an angel, a guardian of hope, in the form of Jonathan Wener, the visionary Chairman of Canderel. Jonathan, like a masterful conductor orchestrating a symphony of fate, introduced me to the late Aaron Fish, Founder and CEO of Unican Security Systems Ltd.

Jonathan had regaled Aaron with a tale of a book we had meticulously crafted for him, a masterpiece that had touched the chords of his heart. The brilliant designer behind this work of art, Sarah Morley of Design Postimage, had also sung my praises, letting Aaron in on the fact that the man behind the magic of print was none other than yours truly.

Aaron, a man of discernment, saw something in me beyond balance sheets and price tags. He entrusted me with a book project, despite the price being a steep fifteen thousand dollars more than what China could offer. Curiosity piqued, I dared to ask him, "Why me?" His response was that his wife had imparted a wisdom that resonated with him. After amassing wealth around the world, she felt it was time to invest back into the heart of Canada. It was no longer about penny-pinching; it was about a higher purpose.

In our fleeting encounters, Aaron had glimpsed the echoes of my rollercoaster career, a journey mirroring his own in many ways. He began to harbour a fondness for me, and expressed that I reminded him of a younger version of himself.

On one unforgettable morning, I emailed Aaron at 5 a.m. To my surprise, he replied back almost immediately and we met later that morning. Little did I know that this rendezvous would become another pivotal chapter in my life's narrative. Ever the maestro of unexpected opportunities, Aaron invited me to purchase his expansive large-format company.

In the quiet solitude of dawn, Aaron disclosed his audacious plan: he would loan me half a million dollars, and with this financial lifeline, I was to purchase shares of his large-format company for two hundred thousand dollars, settle an equal sum of my debts, and allocate a hundred thousand dollars to steer the business toward a triumphant future. Yet, the catch was that he would charge me five percent interest, with the principal amount payable when circumstances permitted.

As Aaron's words hung in the air, I found myself utterly speechless, overwhelmed to the core. I was awash with emotions, and I could barely contain them. Tears streamed down my cheeks as I sat in my car, grappling with the sheer incredulity of it all. This was a serious deal - an offer almost too good to be true! Of course I accepted – with great gratitude.

This opportunity allowed me to level-up Pazazz's capabilities beyond my wildest dreams.

Now, let's take a moment to bask in the glory of some remarkable firsts that my business proudly boasts. We've always been driven by the audacious pursuit of excellence, and it shows.

We were trailblazers, the pioneers of our field. While others were content treading the familiar paths, we set our sights on uncharted territory. We were the first in all of Canada to achieve not one, not two, but three prestigious certifications: FSC, PEFC, and SFC. These weren't just badges on our chest; they were our tickets to the stratosphere of success.

Why bother with competition when you can simply make them irrelevant by soaring in a league of your own? Why swim in the crowded, turbulent red oceans when you can create a whole new blue ocean, where the possibilities are boundless, and the market is yours for the taking?

These audacious moves were nothing short of brilliant. They catapulted us to the forefront of the industry, setting us apart as leaders, innovators, and visionaries. Clients flocked to our banner, eager to be part of a journey that defied convention and embraced a future unburdened by limitations.

* *

The year was 2007, a time when the internet was still finding its footing, and I decided to embark on a digital adventure that would change my life forever.

With a twinkle in my eye and a hint of mischief, I unleashed a video on a little-known platform called YouTube.

Now, let me set the scene. I posted this video for the sheer fun of it, and I kid you not, as I settled back onto my trusty couch, the view count began to skyrocket. First, it was a hundred views, then a thousand, and before I knew it, the numbers were dancing around like hyperactive electrons – 5,000, 10,000, 25,000, and the grand finale, a jaw-dropping 280,000 unique views! And remember, this was the dark ages internet back in 2007.

This video of mine turned me into an overnight sensation. When I strutted into print events, I was hailed as the "print video guy." People clamoured to snap photos with me, and begged to join my network, and I had a simple criterion – give me a hug, and you're in! The titans of the print industry, the big daddies like KBA and Mitsubishi, wanted a piece of the action too. I went on to post videos of KBA, which they loved. In return, they started promoting my KBA installation videos to their potential new customers.

There is no job to small when building your own business. KBA 142 was just installed

So, there you have it, the tale of how a mischievous video and a whole lot of charm turned me into a superstar in the unlikeliest of places – the world of print.

In the next few years, I embarked on a whirlwind journey through various industry associations and trade bodies. From the Entrepreneur Organization to the Xerox Premier Partners and industry peer groups, I was riding a wave of opportunities, levelling up my game as an industry expert and a recognized authority in the field.

But as life has a knack for reminding us, stability in business is a fleeting mirage. The winds of change began to blow in 2018, and we found ourselves losing some colossal accounts. It was a brutal wake-up call, a stark reminder that in the world of business, change is the only constant. We watched in dismay as our cherished accounts slipped through our fingers, impacting our steady flow of a staggering US$ 2,000,000 in business. The weight of that loss sent shockwaves through our company.

Money grew tighter, squeezing us into a financial vice. And if that wasn't enough, a devastating blow struck. While I was back at the bank to restructure the company, it turns out that my business partner, along with my President, were planning a takeover.

But the storm didn't stop there; it raged on for the next 18 relentless months. In January 2019, I found myself out of business, staring at a bleak horizon. Tragedy compounded tragedy as sixty days later, in March 2019, my mother passed away after a gruelling six-month illness. And as if life were intent on piling on the agony, I lost my mother-in-law in May 2019 – another short sixty days later.

With a heavy heart and a battered spirit, I had planned a reset – a six month escape into the solace of fishing, a chance to distance myself from the turmoil of whatever BS life wanted to continue throwing at me. But fate had other plans. My beloved Ranger boat and trailer, second only to my children, was stolen. It was a cruel twist of fate that left me reeling.

Amid this chain of events, the world plunged into the grip of the COVID-19 pandemic. The turmoil in my personal life continued as well, when my fiancée left me, and our relationship of eight years ended. Stress consumed me, and I felt like I was drowning in a sea of challenges. One hit after another, no reprieve in sight, no time to recover.

In the midst of this maelstrom, a glimmer of hope emerged. A recommendation led me to Ellie Ballantine (www. ellieballentine.com), a life coach who would become my sounding board. She helped me navigate the treacherous waters, teaching me to reconfigure and rewire myself. The most profound lesson was the power of meditation, the belief in the simple act of breathing to regain control. It's been a few years, and I still consult with Ellie every month, a lifeline in my journey of healing and growth.

Now, you may be wondering, what am I up to these days? Well, it was during the throes of the pandemic that I decided to pay it forward. I wanted to help others with what I'd learned from my tumultuous experiences - and The Print Whisperer was born. While I still dabble in print, I no longer engage with those looking to haggle over quotes. Instead, I offer my expertise and provide genuine value - a an Ellie-inspired haven for small to mid-sized print business owners and managers across the global print industry.

Why? Because I've walked in their shoes, and I know the challenges they face every single day. How? Driven by innovation and fuelled by the thrill of a good challenge, I offer a candid, positive, and famously exuberant approach to dissecting operations, revitalizing sales processes, streamlining production workflows, and revamping marketing strategies.

I know that owner-to-owner is a different kind of conversation.

Roots and Beginnings

In retrospect, when I think about my journey into the wild and wacky world of the print industry, I can't help but chuckle. You see, it all started with my father, who ran a small print shop. As a kid, I watched him wake up at the crack of dawn to head to work. He did whatever he did in there (I still think he was secretly printing money), but it was all to keep the family show running.

Now, my initial impression of the print industry wasn't exactly love at first sight. I mean, who in their right mind wants to get their hands dirty with ink stains and grease? Not me, that's for sure. But fate had other plans. On my very first day at my father's company, I randomly picked a company from the Yellow Pages, hoping for a small miracle. I struck gold – or, in this case, a cool $2700 label order for a women's hair product company. My very first foray into sales, and I was winning like a champ! I started doing the math in my head, dreaming of swimming in cash – $70,200 a year, to be precise (considering a 10% incentive – 270 X 5 days X 52 weeks) But, alas, life had different plans, and for the next few months, I couldn't land another order if my life depended on it.

My stint in the sales department turned out to be a wild adventure. I met people from all walks of life, from furniture manufacturers to helicopter-making wizards. Yes, you read that right, I toured a helicopter factory – it was like my very own episode of "How Do You Make That?" The memories of that day are etched in my mind like a printer etches ink on paper.

As the years went by, I realized I couldn't be a master of all trades. I didn't quite grasp the art of estimating, and machines and I had a mutual agreement – I wouldn't touch them, and they wouldn't confuse me. So, I happily stayed in sales.

My family was over the moon to see the shift in my priorities. Instead of my carefree teenage days, which were filled with motorcycling adventures and hanging out with friends, I had transformed into someone who couldn't wait to dive into the world of print each day. While my peers were still chasing the thrill of the latest video games or partying till dawn, I was burning the midnight oil, discussing the intricacies of print and the joy of my achievements, big and small. You could say I was the odd one out, but I wore my newfound passion like a badge of honour.

Now, let's fast forward to a moment that tugs at my heartstrings - my first four-colour, 16-page catalogue. It's a memory that's woven with gratitude and respect for a man named Peter Rollit from Montreal, who had a trusty 20 X 26, 4-color Komori press. Our paths crossed when an unexpected ice storm disrupted his business plans. Little did we know that this twist of fate would turn him into a mentor and a trusted problem solver, leaving an indelible mark on our journey. He later joined our business and we worked together until his last breath.

My brother and I sat on the shopfloor of Peter's factory, watching page after page of our catalogue roll off the press, it was like witnessing a masterpiece in the making. There were no fancy computer-to-plate systems back then, just the craft of burning negatives and plates, and the alchemy of four-colour printing. The emotions that swelled within me were a mix of awe, appreciation, and the realization that we were part of something truly special. It was a pivotal moment that solidified our passion for print and our commitment to this extraordinary industry.

But let's rewind for a moment to my teenage years, where life was a thrilling rollercoaster of quirky interests. You see, I had a knack for noticing the most unconventional things, like those intriguing lingerie inserts that piqued the curiosity of any teenager. It was like a secret treasure hunt, and who could resist a bit of mystery?

And then there were the magazines and comic books that fuelled my youthful imagination. Batman and Superman swooped into my world, making me dream of superpowers and epic adventures. The misadventures of the gang from Archies provided a dose of teenage drama and humour, while MAD magazine had me in stitches with its zany humour. But let's not forget the car magazines, where the sleek designs and horsepower figures had my heart racing faster than a sports car on an open road. And, of course, there was Playboy – a forbidden fruit for a teenager, with its glossy finish, vibrant colours, and pin-sharp resolutions that brought sensuality to life on every page.

My teenage years were a collage of visual experiences, each page a portal to another world, another adventure. Little did I know that this fascination with visuals would later lead me to an industry where every detail, every image, and every colour would come together to create magic on paper.

As the years rolled on, my print sales soared to new heights. From a humble beginning of $327,000 in the first year, I was already feeling the thrill of success. But it was only the beginning of this exhilarating journey.

In the second year, we made a giant leap, and our sales rocketed to an impressive $725,000. The passion and determination that fuelled my every step were unwavering. And the excitement was just getting started.

In the third year, we shattered all expectations, achieving a whopping $1,035,000 in sales. It was like riding the most thrilling rollercoaster imaginable, with every twist and turn marking another victory.

I was over the moon and, driven by a clear vision, I started dreaming big. I meticulously mapped out our path to success in a detailed Excel spreadsheet, planning for the next 15 years. I could see our growth unfolding before my eyes. By the time we reached our 12th year, the dream turned into a reality as we hit the astonishing milestone of $15 million. It was a testament to the power of manifestation, unwavering passion, and the undeniable direction that had guided me through this incredible journey.

I had transformed our small venture into a corporation, and we were beaming with pride. I'd meet clients and tell them,

"I just want to earn some money, get married, have kids, and enjoy life." It was all about sales, but our clients loved it. We were the "here they come" duo, brimming with ideas, hard work, and most importantly, fun.

For all you aspiring print enthusiasts, I have one piece of advice – start looking for print everywhere around you. It's in the boxes shipped by Amazon, on cartons, inserts, product labels, manuals, brochures, leaflets – you name it. Once you really see it – you suddenly see print everywhere. It's all about perception and noticing what's already around you.

The print industry has evolved significantly, and technology is its best buddy. Youngsters will be fascinated by the tech-edge this industry now offers. With a few clicks, you can process print, match colours, and witness magic on various substrates. The results are so sharp that they're almost like works of art. Everything has to be picture-perfect – it's not just about print quality; it's the finishing touches that truly make a difference. Think embossed, debossed, UV-raised effects on product packaging to elevate your brand.

I hope you take away a few things from my journey. First and foremost, don't be afraid to explore different industries until you find your "Ikigai" – your reason to live and work. Steve Jobs once said, "Your work is going to fill a large part of your life, and the only way to be truly satisfied is to do what you believe is great work." So, keep searching, keep believing, and don't settle. And always remember, it's not just about what you do but also how you do it; it's about finding what sets your heart on fire.

Changing Moments

Once upon a time, in the bustling kingdom of business where the printers roared and the deadlines loomed like oversized towers, I stumbled upon a rare gem – the intricate dance of people management. In the vast savannah of commerce, we often find ourselves armed with the mightiest of tools – technology, foolproof processes, and the sacred scrolls of KRAs and KPIs. Yet, in the midst of this, we tend to overlook the wild, unpredictable beasts that roam our corporate landscapes – the human workforce, prone to changing behaviours and attitudes.

Let me regale you with a tale, a saga where my prowess in managing the human zoo was put to the ultimate test. Imagine this: a relatively small printing empire with a Plant Manager who wasn't just a manager; he was the maestro orchestrating the symphony of our operations. He became my go-to guy for everything under the printing sun, earning the coveted title of the Jack of All Trades. In a fit of entrepreneurial intensity, I once declared, "You will be with me for life!"

Fast forward to a moment of awakening – a realization that I was holding onto him like a tattered security blanket. The business had evolved, systems were in place, and his once-mighty contribution now felt like a rusty cog in the printing machine. Ah, the pitfalls of commitment echoing louder than reason. Ever been in a situation where trust and empowerment blur the line between necessity and sentiment? I bet I have touched upon some hidden corners of your entrepreneurial heart.

So, there I sat, in a predicament, pondering how to delicately release my Plant Manager from the clutches of corporate servitude, especially after making commitments that sounded more permanent than a tattoo. Lesson learned: Everyone is replaceable, and no one is indispensable.

Enter the sage wizard of my business odyssey – Peter Rollit. Why was I so drawn to Peter? Ten years my senior, he possessed a young mind, a repository of knowledge, and an uncanny ability to infuse warmth into any conversation. A family man at heart, every dialogue with his wife and his kids dripped with a thousand "I love yous." His gift to me, a caliper passed down from his father, is a cherished relic and tangible reminder of our shared journey.

Peter, my Yoda in the print galaxy, was a maestro of business strategy; under his guardianship, I learned the art of differentiation – a skill that would set our printing enterprise on an extraordinary trajectory. Our journey resembled a cosmic dance, a waltz with industry giants like Pfizer, where every step was a stroke of ingenuity.

In the pulsating rhythm of our meeting room, we harnessed the spirit of competition and survival, embedding it into our pitch to Pfizer. Our high-stakes presentation to the pharmaceutical titan was inspired by the dynamics of the "Survivor" show – a reality TV phenomenon where contestants must outwit, outlast, and outplay to emerge victorious.

Peter, with his seasoned wisdom, understood the power of storytelling in business. He believed that a compelling narrative could transform a transaction into a partnership, a client into an ally. Our Survivor-inspired presentation wasn't just a showcase of printing capabilities; it was a narrative that spoke to the core values of our potential clients, forging a connection beyond the area of business.

No ordinary presentation, it was a theatrical performance, a symphony of words and visuals that captivated our audience, leaving an indelible mark on the minds of Pfizer decision-makers. This venture into unconventional storytelling was a bold leap, a departure from the mundane boardroom presentations that echoed in the corporate hallways.

This endeavour, inspired by the Survivor ethos, taught me a fundamental lesson in the annals of my entrepreneurial education – to stand out, one must dare to be different. It wasn't merely about showcasing our printing capabilities; it was about crafting a narrative that resonated and lingered in the minds of our clients. In the cutthroat world of business, where monotony often reigns, our presentation was a breath of fresh air, a testament to our commitment to innovation.

The Survivor analogy wasn't just a gimmick; it was a philosophy that permeated our approach to every project. We adopted the Survivor mindset – strategic thinking to outwit competitors, resilience to outlast challenges, and a relentless pursuit of excellence to outplay the status quo. It became a rallying cry for our team, a mantra that fueled our creative endeavours.

As the Survivor-inspired strategy unfolded, it became a touchstone for our future endeavours. We sought inspiration not just from the conventional norms of the printing industry but from diverse sources – reality shows, literature, and art. This approach transformed our business into a canvas of creativity, where every project became an opportunity to weave a unique narrative.

In the grand platform of business, the Survivor-inspired presentation was a vibrant thread, contributing to the rich narrative of our entrepreneurial journey. It wasn't just a strategy; it was a mindset that echoed in our approach to challenges, a philosophy that celebrated the beauty of being different.

So, in the world of print and business, as we waltzed with giants and etched our story, the Survivor-inspired lesson became a guiding light. Outwit, outlast, and outplay – not just as a strategic move but as a philosophy that breathed life into our entrepreneurial spirit. And in that dance with industry titans, we discovered that standing out wasn't just about ink and paper; it was about weaving narratives that resonated in the hearts of our clients, ensuring that our story became an unforgettable chapter in the annals of the print galaxy.

We didn't get the pharma account, but the lessons learned were priceless. In our sprint through the business marathon, we never turned down a challenge. Retrospectively, did our eagerness to embrace every project hamper our business? The jury's still out, but we reveled in the thrill of relentless deadlines. I often questioned the sanity of clients demanding a Friday delivery on a Wednesday or needing something at 9 a.m. on a Monday. My solution: deliver by noon on Monday and use the weekend wisely.

Yet, as the dust settled on another hectic workday, I found myself pondering FedEx duties. My wife's retort, and beacon of wisdom was, "Work towards a day when someone else in your company will do that for you." A priceless lesson: Systems and processes were not just fancy jargon; they were the gears of efficient business machinery.

Ah, the systems. Estimations on Excel, shipping memos on Word, and our trusty MIS named Avanti kept the wheels turning. Then came the upheaval – the Avanti Classic to Slingshot upgrade that left my company in a sea of bugs. The transition was brutal, but amidst the chaos, a silver lining emerged – free access as the sounding board for Avanti Slingshot's improvements.

Change, however, is a bitter pill to swallow. Witnessing the struggle of my team, I delved into the intricate dance of scaling a business. With no formal printing background or academic laurels, I became a perpetual learner. Three decades in, I'm still at it. Networking became my Excalibur, a potent weapon that stood the test of time. I joined forums, and associations, and hobnobbed at various networking events – a business owner's treasure trove.

But my most remarkable move was a peer group, a council of wise business wizards with whom I could discuss anything, from buying machines to vendor selection. Networking wasn't just a buzzword; it was my secret sauce, leading to fruitful collaborations and business opportunities. Navigating the diverse waters of networking, I charted my course through institutions and charitable organizations like NAPL (National Association for Printing & Leadership), Idealliance, combined Jewish Appeal, the Juvenile Diabetes Foundation and the Montreal Children's Hospital Foundation. These weren't mere gatherings; they were treasure troves of opportunities waiting to be unearthed. Networking wasn't just about handshakes and business cards; it was about collaboration, helping others, engaging and cultivating meaningful connections that transcended the boundaries of industry. With an open-minded attitude and vigilant senses, I discovered that opportunities for a printer abound in unexpected places. It wasn't just about being in the right rooms; it was about being receptive to the possibilities that echoed through every interaction and engagement. Print is all around. You have to look for it.

So, dear reader, let this be a whimsical, insightful journey into the world of entrepreneurship. In this discord of lessons, remember: everyone is replaceable, embrace differentiation, and for the love of all things print, network like your business depends on it.

Balancing Work and Life

In the golden era of running my print business, my days were like a blockbuster movie. The day started at the crack of dawn, a symphony of whirring machines, and the occasional ink-stained superhero swooping in with the grace of a caffeinated cat. My working hours were a rollercoaster ride – six in the morning to eight in the evening, Monday to Friday, with a dash of weekend warrior-ing thrown in. Ah, the good ol' days when the printers hummed, and I waltzed with paper reams. While I was obviously enjoying all this, I wondered, was I missing out on something?

As my kids transitioned from the innocence of bedtime stories to the complexities of growing up, my role in their lives faced a profound shift. Once the orchestrator of their bedtime tales, I found myself on the sidelines as my wife took the lead in navigating the maze of their evolving needs. The demands of the printing industry, with its relentless rhythm, often echoed the organized chaos of their teenage years. Yet, amidst the relentless pulse of the printing press, I clung fiercely to a promise – to be there for every spectacle of their lives.

The crescendo of school gatherings and ballet recitals became the heartbeats of my commitment. It was a vow etched into the very fabric of my being, a promise to witness the magic of tiny humans performing grand acts of cuteness. If family sentiment could be quantified, I'd like to believe I'd score high. My entrances, though occasionally causing a stir, were my signature – a fashionably late arrival, eyes fixed on me as I sauntered in. Embarrassment may have lingered in the air, but the entertainment value was undeniable. In those moments, amid the applause and laughter, I discovered the true art of balancing life's grand performances with the relentless demands of owning a business.

Jonathan & Annie today

In the hustle of the first ten years, the printing business, known for its unpredictable deadlines and peculiar demands, felt like a wild show – and I was its star performer. I was often expected to be a magician, producing finished products with just a wave of my printing wand, with the audience believeing that as soon as ink touched paper, the invisible printing magic would ensure a quick and flawless delivery. Trying to explain the delicate steps of drying, finishing, and packing was often performed against the backdrop of unrealistic expectations. So, in the middle of this captivating act, the idea of instant creation stuck around, forcing me to navigate the demanding stage with a mix of skill and resilience.

In the rhythm of my entrepreneurial journey, a vital lesson unfolded – the importance of rest. It wasn't just a luxury but a fundamental necessity. The brain, much like a fine wine, requires moments to breathe, allowing the flavours of creativity to mature and evolve. A chaotic and relentless schedule, much like a vigorously shaken soda can, eventually loses its fizz. The incessant demands and pressures, if unattended, can severely impact the quality of both your output and decision-making capabilities.

I discovered that carving out time for relaxation and moments of stillness acted as a reset button for my mind. It was during these pauses that the seeds of innovative ideas were planted and allowed to germinate. The creative process, much like nature, requires its seasons – moments of dormancy followed by periods of vibrant growth. Embracing this natural rhythm became pivotal for sustaining a dynamic and thriving business.

Enter the consulting domain – a role where the cards are played differently and the schedule is mine to control. The day begins at six, because apparently, I've forgotten how to sleep in. After some bed contemplation, the day kicks off with meditation, hitting a step count that would make any fitness tracker proud, and a gym session. By 9 a.m, breakfast is conquered, and I seamlessly transit to my home office, a place of online meetings, client visits, phone calls, reading escapades, creative brainstorming, and whatnot.

In carefully planned trips, each detail plays a special role, crafting memorable moments. The getaway with my wife, a refuge tucked away from the demands of daily life, echoed with whispers of shared secrets and laughter. The setting, carefully chosen for its seclusion, allowed us to disconnect from the hustle and immerse ourselves in a cocoon of undisturbed togetherness. As the sun dipped below the horizon, painting the sky in hues of orange and pink, our conversations meandered through the realms of dreams and nostalgia.

With the kids in tow, our getaways transformed into kaleidoscopic adventures – from lively resorts to sun-kissed beaches and the exhilarating slopes of skiing destinations. Each escapade was a canvas where we painted memories in the vibrant strokes of family bonds. The resorts echoed with the laughter of my children, their joyous exclamations bouncing off the walls. We delved into the simplicity of building sandcastles, the thrill of gliding down snowy slopes, and the warmth of shared stories around a crackling bonfire.

The solo getaway, a ritual of solitude amidst the serene artistry of nature, offered a profound connection with my inner self. Fishing became a metaphorical journey – a dance between patience and anticipation. The quietude of the still water mirrored the tranquility I sought, a sanctuary for introspection. Beneath the open sky, I found solace in the simplicity of the moment, the rhythmic sounds of nature composing a melody that resonated with the quiet corners of my soul.

These carefully curated getaways were not merely vacations; they were a deliberate investment in the treasury of family bonds and personal rejuvenation. The nature that surrounded us in these getaways became a silent yet powerful participant, influencing the tenor of our interactions and infusing each memory with the magic of its own rhythm. In those stolen moments of quality time, I discovered that the best version of myself emerged outside the cacophony of deadlines, and within the harmonious cadence of shared laughter, quiet reflections, and the embracement of nature.

In my entrepreneurial journey, the vibrant threads of inspiration were woven by two extraordinary individuals, namely, Dave

Harding and Larry Kendel. Dave, the technological virtuoso at Harding Poorman, orchestrated a factory that mirrored the precision of a NASA laboratory. His commitment to cutting-edge technology, innovative processes, and a revolutionary profit-sharing approach transformed his business into a well-oiled machine, with motivated and engaged personnel.

Warren looking at a press sheet

On the other hand, Larry Kendel, a second-generation printer and luminary behind Cameocraft, showcased an unparalleled mastery in human connection. As we walked the floor of his bustling factory, I was struck by his ability to address each of his hundred employees by their first name. This personal touch resonated throughout his business, emphasizing the profound impact effective communication can have on relationships and, subsequently, on the triumphs of a business. Their unwavering commitment and dedication were like beacons guiding me through the intricate waters of entrepreneurship.

The illumination cast by Dave and Larry in my entrepreneurial saga isn't merely a tale of industry prowess; it's a testament to the significance of relationships in the intricate dance between work and life. Beyond the whirring machinery and the scent of ink, the core of our endeavors is human connection. Work and life, intricately entwined, each influencing the other in a rhythmic synergy. These luminaries serve as beacons not only because they mastered the art of printing - but because they excelled in the art of relationships.

Installation of KBA 142 2008

Why does this matter? Your work mirrors your character – a canvas painted with respect or disregard. Treating others well in the workplace isn't distinctive from treating family and friends well at home; it's a seamless integration. The boundaries blur, blend, and harmonize. The pandemic, in its turbulence, became a powerful instructor, guiding us towards a deeper understanding of what truly matters.

The pandemic's lessons resonate – family takes precedence, personal moments are sacrosanct, and the artistry of navigating work and life defies the rigidity of science. COVID, with its disruptive force, laid bare the fragility of assumed certainties. Amidst the chaos, the fundamental truth emerged –

relationships, whether within the family or the professional world, form the bedrock of our lives. It taught us the irreplaceable value of human connection, the necessity of moments with loved ones, and the ability to weave work and life into a seamless, meaningful world.

New 56" Fuji CTP just installed

These lessons echo through the corridors of retrospection, reminding us that every challenge, every inkblot, and every laughter-filled break contributes to the unique canvas of our journey. The essence lies in triumphs and resilience - cultivated through failures, in moments of vulnerability, and in the profound connections forged in the crucible of work and life.

Navigating life's intricate choreography, let us carry forward the imprints of wisdom on paper and memories. May humour accompany us, a constant companion lighting even the darkest corners. In life's masterpiece, let hope persist as the backdrop, assuring us that each new dawn unveils a fresh canvas, inviting us to paint a story uniquely our own.

* *

"You probably don't want maximum effectiveness.

For example, the most effective way to make money likely requires a lifestyle you don't want to live. Instead, you want the most effective path that fits your desired lifestyle.

How do you want to spend your days? Start there, then optimize."

James Clear

The Art and Science of Printing

"If all printers were determined not to print anything till they were sure it would offend nobody, there would be very little printed"
Benjamin Franklin – *www.quotefancy.com*

In the world of printing, where each day dances to its own choreography, there comes a moment that rattles the very core of every printer's existence – a project that sends shivers down your spine. Allow me to unfold not one, but two such heart-stopping tales that left an indelible mark on the canvas of my printing journey.

The first - a Christmas Greeting Card project for Fruits & Passion. At first glance, not a behemoth in terms of volume, but oh, the devil was in the details. From navigating the intricate colours, registration challenges, and meticulous printing process, to the pièce de résistance – the die. This wasn't just any die; it was a complicated marvel that set us back a hefty 3000 Canadian dollars. Little did I foresee that a project, seemingly innocent in size, would unleash a seismic wave through our shop floor. The die-cutting demanded a level of finesse that rivaled a surgeon's precision, interlocking the board seamlessly into the shape of a Christmas tree. Have you ever encountered a project so intricate? Trust me, it can push you to the limits of your craft.

And then there was the project that arrived hot on the heels of installing our 56-inch UV Offset press, a machine so rare in our vicinity that news of its arrival spread like wildfire for 500 miles. Enter a gentleman with a proposition to print on plastic – a staggering 500,000 sheets. Brimming with exuberance, I boldly declared, "We can do it!" The project got the green light, budgeted at a cool 83,000 Canadian dollars. The sheet size? A formidable 30 X 42, 15-point PET. The catch? We had never ventured into the world of printing on plastic before.

Calculations were made, relying on the machine's capacity to print 13,500 sheets per hour. A presumed 50 to 60 hours of runtime, a three-week print extravaganza. Little did we know, surprises lurked around the corner.

The job, it turned out, had minimal ink coverage – a mere 5%. Ink, with such sparse coverage, flirted with defiance, refusing to adhere to the sheet. We had to dial back the speed to a painstaking 4000 sheets per hour, extending the project to a daunting 130 hours. A formidable test of our mettle, a challenge that pushed our limits. Fortunately, the client was well aware of the hurdles and, in a way, was testing our resilience. I recalculated the price, presenting him with a revised quote of 133,000 Canadian dollars. The client, savvy to the game, had anticipated this and had based his subsequent negotiations on this new reality. All said and done, everyone walked away content, but not without imbibing a master lesson.

As we navigate the twists and turns of these gripping tales, I'll unravel more lessons learned at the end of this chapter, lessons etched in the crucible of real-world challenges and triumphs in the printing industry.

* *

Transitioning from the helm of my own press to my current role as a Consultant, I've retained a cardinal principle: keep your ears firmly on the ground. It's a mantra that echoes louder than ever in an industry where evolution is the norm. Staying attuned to the industry's heartbeat, understanding the cadence of competition, and deciphering the ever-shifting symphony of customer trends have been my compass.

Dscoop 2024

In the ever-changing landscape of the printing industry, staying relevant isn't just a personal endeavour — it's a collective responsibility. To this end, I've been a steadfast attendee of industry forums, a loyal patron of trade shows, a subscriber to the pulsating alerts from industry websites, and, perhaps most crucially, a curator of face-to-face rendezvous with the maestros behind the machines—the manufacturers.

Trade shows aren't merely events; they are the lifeblood of our industry in my opinion. It's not just about their survival; it's about the industry's survival. A pilgrimage to these exhibitions is more than a professional obligation; it's a commitment to prop up the very ecosystem we thrive in. Here, amidst the booths and banners, relationships are forged, insights gleaned, and the collective pulse of the industry felt.

Podcasting has become another arrow in my quiver. Leveraging my extensive network, I've assumed the role of a bridge — connecting the visionaries crafting the next generation of printing machinery with the astute buyers seeking technological marvels. Each episode unfolds as a narrative, a dialogue that transcends the auditory to offer tangible takeaways for all stakeholders.

But let's go further, where every handshake, every nod of acknowledgment, and every uttered word transcends the mundane and transforms into a nuanced dance of industry dynamics.

Trade Shows: A Platform of Industry Vibrancy

Imagine a bustling trade show—the vibrant hum of conversations, the rhythmic thud of machines in operation, and the kaleidoscope of innovation unfolding in every corner. This is not just a congregation of professionals; it's a celebration of progress, a testament to the resilience of an industry perpetually on the move. Today, machines are not on display as they were earlier and not loud enough to make your heart beat heavily nor are machine manufacturers getting equipment either.

When I step onto the trade show floor, it's not merely as a participant; it's a pilgrimage to the beating heart of my profession. The tangible energy pulsating through the booths is infectious. It's where dreams materialize into prototypes, and prototypes metamorphose into the next industry revolution.

There's an inherent thrill in meeting the minds behind the machines. The engineers and innovators, fueled by a passion to redefine the possibilities of print. These encounters transcend the transactional; they are the genesis of partnerships that propel the industry forward.

But amidst the gleaming machines and polished pitches, there's an intangible treasure — the collective wisdom of industry veterans. It's in the stories exchanged over coffee, the anecdotes shared during a workshop, and the camaraderie forged in the crucible of shared challenges. Here, in this cacophony of innovation, relationships are the unsung heroes, the invisible threads weaving the industry's future.

Podcasting: Harmonizing Industry Voices

As a podcaster, I've found a unique avenue to amplify these industry voices. The microphone becomes a conduit for narratives that transcend the confines of boardrooms and workshops. Each episode unfolds as a tableau, capturing the essence of innovation, the pulse of market trends, and the foresight of industry leaders.

In these conversations, manufacturers aren't merely suppliers; they are storytellers, narrating the genesis of their creations. The whir of the printing press becomes a backdrop to tales of challenges overcome, innovations embraced, and the relentless pursuit of perfection. It's a sonic journey into the heart of the machinery, where every gear has a story to tell.

But the podcast isn't a monologue; it's a dialogue that extends beyond the recording studio. It's a shared space where manufacturers elucidate the nuances of their craft, and buyers glean insights that transcend the glossy brochures. The podcast isn't just a broadcast; it's a symphony where each note contributes to the collective melody of the industry.

The Takeaway: A Symphony of Industry Resilience

In this ever-evolving symphony of the printing industry, every note, every chord, and every pause contributes to the larger composition. The trade shows, the podcasts, the face-to-face interactions — they are not isolated endeavours but interconnected strands weaving the scope of our profession.

So, as I continue to traverse these worlds, where the echoes of innovation reverberate and industry stalwarts share their wisdom, I urge every practitioner to join this symphony. Attend the trade shows, amplify your voice through podcasts, and, most importantly, embrace the relationships that form the backbone of our industry.

For in this harmonious collaboration lies the resilience of our craft, the adaptability to industry shifts, and the promise of a future where the printing press, in all its glory, continues to script stories of progress and innovation.

* *

In the world of print, where creativity intertwines with design and execution, it's akin to orchestrating a symphony of colours, shapes, and precision. The printing industry is graced with the presence of creative minds that can weave visual tales, but therein lies a potential pitfall—design and execution can sometimes be distant relatives, and this uneasy alliance can spell disaster. Let me unravel the strategies we employed to navigate this delicate dance, minimizing challenges and ensuring a seamless process.

First and foremost, I instilled the practice of being summoned for discussions and project inspections at the design stage. It wasn't merely a power move; it was a strategic initiative to impart insights, often gratuitously, on what's feasible, what aligns with the project goals, and what might be a potential stumbling block. This proactive involvement not only earned us brownie points but, more importantly, set the stage for cost savings that could be achieved by establishing well-defined ground rules. Whether it was the hues selected, the dimensions of branding, finishing touches, folding techniques, cutting intricacies, or the finer points of packing, every detail mattered, and addressing them at the inception was akin to laying a sturdy foundation.

In our arsenal of tactics, crafting mock-ups and prototypes emerged as a potent weapon. Even an unfinished version, labeled as "Version One," trumped venturing into the unknown. It was a testament to the philosophy that a tangible representation, no matter how rudimentary, could serve as a compass, steering us away from potential pitfalls. After all, in the world of print, it's often better to iterate and refine in the laboratory of prototypes than to shoot in the dark, hoping for perfection on the first attempt.

Client approvals at pivotal junctures became a non-negotiable prerequisite in our workflow. Press passes, dummy approvals, meticulous corrections — each step was a crucial checkpoint. We considered a signed proof not just as a piece of paper but as a legally binding document, a contract delineating the agreed-upon specifications. It was an educational journey for the clients, as not everyone comprehended the gravity of a signed proof. The print world, with its millions of sheets produced daily, couldn't afford to meticulously comb through every page in the final output. It might sound harsh, but this was our reality.

Navigating the treacherous aftermath of project hiccups requires finesse and resilience. Imagine this - the final sheets have rolled off the presses, and the finish line appears within grasp, but a lingering misstep threatens to unravel the entire hard work. In these tumultuous moments, the scenes can indeed turn ugly. Heated arguments, akin to a tempest, whirl around, threatening to dismantle the collaborative effort. Negotiations over revised prices unfold, a delicate dance where the equilibrium must be restored without compromising the integrity of the project. Material wastages, a silent casualty, add to the financial toll, and reworkings plunge the team back into the trenches, revisiting stages deemed completed. Missed deadlines, the ultimate sin in the printing world, cast a looming shadow over the entire operation. Each delayed tick of the clock not only amplifies the financial strain but also tarnishes the reputation carefully built over years. The repercussions of these missteps are akin to a ripple effect, touching not only the immediate project but also casting shadows on future collaborations.

Amid this chaos, the crucial lifeline is clear communication and client education. Transparency becomes the beacon guiding both parties through the storm. It's a time to pause, assess, and recalibrate expectations. Clients, too, are embarked on an educational journey, understanding that the intricacies of the printing process extend beyond the surface. The signed proof, once a mere formality, now metamorphoses into a sacred pact, a commitment to shared objectives.

In the quest to surpass customer expectations, printers often find themselves treading a fine line between ambition and presumption. Actions, driven by noble intentions to meet stringent deadlines, can inadvertently become casualties of assumptions. The seemingly innocuous phrase, "I thought it was to be done like this," echoes like a haunting refrain. The interplay between expectation and execution requires a delicate choreography, one that, if not navigated with precision, can lead to a cacophony instead of the harmonious symphony envisioned.

These adversities in the print cosmos serve as lessons etched in the annals of experience. They underscore the importance of meticulous planning, collaborative communication, and a nuanced understanding of the fine balance between design aspirations and the realities of execution. It's a reminder that, in the world of print, every stroke of the brush and every alignment on the canvas is a collective effort, a dance where the partners — creativity, design, and execution—must move in perfect synchrony to create the masterpiece envisioned.

So, in our journey through the print cosmos, we learned that while creativity sets the stage, it's the meticulous marriage of design and execution, punctuated by transparent communication, that truly orchestrates a masterpiece. The process is a ballet of precision, a symphony of colors, and, above all, a collaborative dance between the creators and the bearers of their visual tales.

In the ever-evolving print industry, the environment takes center stage, transforming from a mere backdrop to a dynamic player that demands attention, adaptation, and above all, innovation. Stepping into this arena can indeed be daunting, a swirling dance of challenges and opportunities that beckon printers to not merely survive but thrive.

The print industry, a formidable giant in its own right, navigating the labyrinth of environmental considerations. It's not just a business; it's a reality where every stroke of the printing press becomes a brushstroke on the canvas of sustainability. The buzzword here is adaptation – a metamorphosis that propels the print industry beyond its conventional confines, making environmental consciousness its new differentiator, catapulting ahead of competitors who lag in this transformative race.

Now, let me be candid. While I don't claim expertise in the exhaustive compendium of environmental best practices, I do harbour a strong conviction in their importance, up to a certain point. The raw materials coursing through the veins of print processes have weathered the crucible of stringent tests and embraced good practices. The very fabric of printing — paper — is often adorned with the FSC label, ink adopts the eco-friendly guise of soy-based composition, and the utilization of vegetable inks underscores the commitment to recyclability. Phthalate, once a silent accomplice, is now virtually eradicated from the print-plus items, further diminishing the industry's carbon footprint.

Certificates and accolades abound, from ISOs to Pantone Certifications, and the comprehensive scrutiny of social audits. These badges of honour, while undeniably valuable, sometimes find themselves eclipsed in the eyes of the beholder — the customer. As much as we embrace and champion these certifications, the reality crystallizes—customers, in their nuanced dance of choices, often remain indifferent. It's a revelation that prompts introspection: What truly matters in the delicate balance between environmental stewardship and customer satisfaction?

Here, the sage advice echoes, "Write down what you do and do what you write down." It's a simple yet profound dictum that encapsulates the essence of disciplined systems and processes. Within the intricate folds of the print industry, execution reigns supreme, the time taken to print a job becomes a silent ballet between variables. Consider the interplay of weather — hot and humid conditions versus the crisp chill of colder days. Yes, the paper, akin to a sentient being, undergoes expansion; the inks, entrusted with the task of vibrant manifestation, linger longer, influencing not only the printing process but the delicate cadence of finishing, folding, binding, and even packing.

Every day unfurls as a learning process, an educational odyssey for printers willing to embrace the quirks and nuances of their craft. It's a realization that permeates the industry with a profound truth – mastery and acceptance of these intricacies are the twin keys that unlock the door to progress. The print industry, with its blend of science and artistry, stands at the precipice of evolution. The question that lingers is not whether printers can adapt, but how boldly they can redefine their narrative, turning the challenges posed by environmental considerations into opportunities for innovation, differentiation, and above all, sustainable growth.

* *

Behold, the dazzling star in the firmament of the print industry – the harbinger of zest and zeal, the trend that set the presses on fire: customization and personalization. Enter the stage, Variable Data Printing (VDP), a maestro orchestrating a symphony of tailored wonders, and the greatest beneficiaries? None other than the illustrious direct mailers and the trailblazing direct marketing industry.

But let me whisk you away to a state where personalization isn't merely a mundane term; it's the sensation of witnessing your name gracefully dance upon the stage of a bespoke product. Look at this: an inbox inundated with a deluge of emails, each brazenly adorned with your name. A collective yawn, a swift click into the void of digital oblivion – such is the fate of these pixelated messengers. Yet, conjure the joy of clasping a mailer, your name etched on its surface like a bespoke poem, or an offer wrapped in the elegance of a neatly printed box, bearing the badge of your identity. Ah, the tactile ecstasy, a desktop calendar proudly flaunting your picture and name, boldly declaring its immunity from the ignominious fate of the nearest dustbin.

An email may waltz into the deletion, or worse, face the cold shoulder of ignorance, but a physical marvel adorned with your name? That's a keepsake, an artifact that transcends the transient nature of virtual correspondence. In a world inundated with the ephemeral glow of screens, the allure of a tangible, personalized creation is not just a whisper; it's a resounding crescendo that captures attention, admiration, and perhaps, a coveted spot on the mantle of cherished possessions. With technology galloping in the digital printing space, the fun has just begun.

* *

Well, well, well, my printing comrades, as we bid adieu to this chapter, it's time to uncork the essence of the printer that courses through my veins. I'm your humble narrator, donned in a printer's cape, ready to share the gospel of ink and paper.

Now, listen up, my printing disciples, for these golden nuggets are the compass to navigate the labyrinth of presses and pitfalls.

First and foremost, let's talk about the moolah – pricing. It's the captain of your ship; get it right, chart your course, and let that treasure chest jingle with the sweet sound of profit. Remember, in this wild printing jungle, there's often no second chance, just like that time when I danced with pricing peril.

Ah, quality, the unsung hero. Define it, embrace it, and make it your loyal companion. If you can't deliver something that's acceptable, take a step back, my friend. Quality is the currency that buys you a seat at the table of lasting impressions.

Now, onto good practices – the secret handshake of the print brotherhood. Strive to be better, not just for yourself but for everyone sharing this colorful, chaotic canvas. Be the printing Picasso of ethical excellence.

Mother Nature's knocking, and it's time to welcome her aboard. The environment is not a bandwagon; it's a spaceship we're all passengers on. So, gear up, reduce, reuse, recycle – be the eco-warrior the world needs.

Operational efficiency, my dear comrades, is where the gold hides. Dig into the roots, streamline, optimize – for in efficiency lies the key to the treasury of prosperity.

Production, the grand conductor of the printing symphony. Schedule with finesse, leave room for surprises (because they'll sneak in uninvited), and cushion your plans. Remember, not every sheet can be the favourite, and not every client a fan of your magnum opus.

Now, let's talk about the ever-elusive common sense. Here's a secret: asking for help is not a weakness; it's a superpower. In this vast printing cosmos, people love to share their wisdom. So, reach out, my friends, and let the echoes of shared knowledge resonate through the hallowed halls of printers' camaraderie.

As the curtain falls on this chapter, let these commandments be your guiding stars. May your presses hum, your inks dance, and your printers' heartbeat to the rhythm of good sense and printing finesse! Onward, my printing comrades, to the next chapter, where the ink flows, and the paper whispers tales of a thousand impressions.

Last but not the least – take care of your customer, before someone else does.

Navigating Industry Storms and Embracing Change

In the tumultuous journey of entrepreneurship, armed with what one believes is a reservoir of intelligence, we often find ourselves blindsided. The winds of change blow unpredictably, and technological shifts, abrupt customer transitions, and the inadequacies of entrenched processes can leave even the savviest entrepreneurs floundering. Stubbornness, the desire to rest on past laurels, and a reluctance to anticipate change further complicate the landscape. While I certainly don't claim exemption from these pitfalls, I have, at times, played the game wisely – but not without my share of missteps.

Evolution of Technology: A Dance with Progress

The technological metamorphosis in the printing industry has been nothing short of revolutionary, reshaping the very foundations of how we operate. Casting my mind back to the 1980s, the Desktop Publishing Revolution (DTP) marked a seismic shift. Software like Adobe PageMaker heralded a new era, allowing designers to craft layouts digitally. How we once managed without such tools now seems an enigma.

Warren with printed sheets of the IGen5 to match his shirt

The 1990s witnessed the advent of Digital Printing, exemplified by Xerox's DocuTech, a pioneer in short-run printing. Simultaneously, the Computer-to-Plate (CTP) Revolution unfolded, eliminating traditional film-based processes by transferring digital files directly to printing plates. This innovation streamlined workflows and significantly enhanced efficiency in the prepress stage. This advancement improved accuracy, reduced production time, and enhanced overall efficiency in the prepress stage of printing. CTP became a standard technology, streamlining workflows and contributing to the evolution of modern printing processes. From the cromalins, colour keys to now the CTP.

The 2000s brought forth Variable Data Printing, a game-changer for mass mailing and direct marketing. The ability to customize content in printed materials became a key driver in the industry. Print on Demand (POD) technology gained traction, allowing for the production of copies in response to actual demand, transforming the dynamics of book publishing.

Print on Demand (POD) technology started gaining prominence in the late 1990s and early 2000s. The concept of POD involves producing copies of a book or other printed materials in response to actual demand, rather than producing a large quantity in advance. This opened up aspiring authors to explore their writing skills and everyone thought they can become writers and get another best-seller on Amazon.

Early 2000s: Expansion of POD Providers. More POD providers entered the market, offering authors and publishers the ability to print books in small runs or even a single copy, reducing the need for large print runs and inventory.

2010s: Growing Popularity

The popularity of POD continued to grow, and major players like Amazon's Kindle Direct Publishing (KDP) and other platforms provided authors with easy access to POD services. POD has become a mainstream method for publishing books, allowing for cost-effective, on-demand printing, reducing waste, and enabling self-publishing authors to reach a global audience.

Overall, POD technology has revolutionized the publishing industry, providing a more flexible and sustainable approach to book printing and distribution.

2005: Introduction of JDF (Job Definition Format)

JDF becomes a standard for integrating different stages of the printing process, enhancing automation and workflow efficiency.

2010s: 3D Printing for Prototyping

3D printing technologies evolve, becoming more accessible for prototyping in the print industry.

2013: Introduction of High-Speed Inkjet Printing

High-speed inkjet printing technology has become more prominent, enabling faster and more cost-effective production.

2015: Nanographic Printing Technology

Nanographic printing is introduced, combining the qualities of offset and digital printing for high-quality results.

2017: Mass Customization with Digital Print

Advances in digital printing allow for mass customization, catering to individualized content and shorter print runs.

2018: Smart Packaging Integration

Integration of smart packaging technologies, incorporating RFID and NFC, providing interactive and trackable packaging solutions.

2020s: AI and Automation Integration

Increased integration of artificial intelligence and automation for predictive maintenance, quality control, and overall process optimization.

2022: Augmented Reality (AR) in Print

Growing use of augmented reality in print materials, enhancing interactivity and user engagement.

As technology evolved, so did the roles of various stakeholders in the industry – graphic designers, DTP operators, sales forces, machine operators, HR personnel, and even the recycling and financing sectors. However, the pace of adapting to the changing external landscape did not match the zeal with which printers acquired new machines and technologies. The struggle to align with the outside world, especially in terms of managing costs, people, and processes, remains a persistent challenge. Even today, costing is not always executed efficiently, with many printers admitting to occasional missteps in pricing.

2024: AI and AGI

In 2024, the integration of Artificial Intelligence (AI) and the advancement towards Artificial General Intelligence

(AGI) are poised to revolutionize the print industry. AI-driven technologies will streamline production processes, enhance quality control, and personalize print materials at unprecedented levels. With AGI on the horizon, machines will exhibit human-like cognitive abilities, leading to innovative designs, predictive analytics, and seamless automation throughout the print lifecycle. This convergence of AI and AGI promises not just efficiency but also creativity, heralding a new era of dynamic, responsive, and adaptive print solutions.

Costing Conundrum: The Unseen Pitfalls

How many printers can candidly acknowledge that, at some point, they've fumbled with pricing? Understanding the crucial distinction between an estimation and a quote is paramount. Personally, I approached pricing by estimating based on the customer's brief, leaving room to refine the quote after receiving the necessary files. Clarity on costs, a well-defined scope, and transparent goalposts regarding raw materials and delivery formed the foundation of this approach.

Backward calculations and internal improvisations often resulted in higher profits than initially projected during the estimation and quoting phases. It's imperative to convey to customers that printers are not just service providers but brand custodians. The success of their products hinges on the printer's ability to enhance their visual appeal, educational value, and attractiveness. While lawyers charge for rectifying drafting errors, printers often find themselves penalized for mistakes, pressured to offer discounts or, worse, receiving no compensation.

In the domain of packaging printing, a relatively stable stream of continuous business allows for more predictable sales and profits. Once a packaging printer masters the nuances of shades, colors, and materials, the projects tend to stay with them. The ability to continually add value, introduce new techniques, and enhance the product makes them indispensable to clients. They can keep adding value, introduce new techniques like digital embellishments, UV, embossing, braille to make the product better and better.

Competitive Intelligence: A Strategic Game

In a quest to understand my competitors, I devised a unique strategy. I enlisted the help of a Marketing Manager to pose as a potential customer and call nineteen of my closest competitors, inquiring about a special binder. This covert operation yielded valuable insights into their responses, pitches, follow-ups, and even their three best references. The exercise uncovered strengths and weaknesses, providing a goldmine of actionable intelligence. Here's the gold dust I could gather from her at the end of the last call she made:

- How did everyone respond to her calls?

- How was their pitch to her?

- Did they ask the right questions?

- She gave a brief and they quoted on the job.

- How many followed-up? A total of around nine out of the nineteen called and emailed her.

- She voluntarily told them she is exploring with a few more names she's talking to who were competitors amongst each other. She asked for their views on them. How did they all respond to this? Some criticized, some showered praises but many were muted not wanting to comment.

- She asked for their three best references and I got a list of leads – real leads of people with their contact details. Trust me, I didn't call anyone as that would have been unethical.

This was an exercise that gave me tons of insights on what's good to do and what's not.

Well, the NAPL crowned me a genius, showering accolades on my supposed out-of-the-box thinking. My wife, on the other hand, had her suspicions, labeling it "corporate espionage with a touch of genius." I must admit, navigating the fine line between groundbreaking strategy and domestic skepticism became a delicate art form.

As I reveled in the praise from industry experts, my wife, with a bemused smile, would jokingly inquire if my next "out-of-the-box" move involved secret missions and clandestine operations. She envisioned a cloak-and-dagger scenario where I, armed with a printer's invoice and a laser-focused strategic plan, would infiltrate competitors' boardrooms under the guise of a coffee connoisseur. In response, I'd playfully assure her that my genius was strictly confined to the realms of printing and strategic business manoeuvres, assuring her that the espionage rumors were greatly exaggerated. Our dinner conversations turned into lively banter, with her posing as the vigilant domestic detective scrutinizing my every move for signs of covert genius.

The NAPL's recognition, rather than putting the matter to rest, only fueled our family's inside joke. "Genius at Large" became my unofficial title at home, with each new consulting venture accompanied by a wink and a playful nod to the supposed covert operations that lay beneath the surface.

In the end, humor became the adhesive that bound the serious business of consulting with the light-heartedness of family banter. My wife's playful suspicions added a layer of amusement to the accolades, creating a narrative where a printer's brilliance walked hand-in-hand with a touch of espionage, all in good fun. So, the next time I'm hailed as a genius, I'll remember to thank my wife for keeping me grounded, always ready to laugh at the humorous side of industry acclaim.

However, I didn't stop at mere data collection. I talked to most of the nineteen competitors to share the findings, sparking reactions ranging from fury to amusement. This exercise, while unconventional, served as a collective eye-opener for the industry, emphasizing the power of introspection and healthy competition. A few were furious, a few laughed over it but many found this an eye-opener.

Strategic Pricing: Unraveling a Client's Misperception

The intricacies of pricing often lead to misunderstandings between printers and clients. An incident involving a Real Estate company seeking elevator graphics serves as a case in point. When a potential client claimed our price was double that of a competitor, instead of succumbing to panic, I probed deeper. Requesting the specifications of the competitor's quote revealed a crucial omission – the absence of matt lamination. Our explanation emphasized the necessity of lamination for durability, preventing damage from cleaning agents. The client, impressed by our attention to detail, awarded us the deal, debunking the misconception that our price was unjustifiably high.

As a Consultant and Coach to numerous printers, my role transcends mere dictation; it involves fostering realization and foresight. I don't impose directives; rather, I become their sounding board, guiding them through a collaborative journey of self-discovery. My aim is to empower printers to see beyond the immediate challenges and envision the broader landscape.

Fostering Self-Realization:

I believe in the transformative power of self-realization. By prompting printers to confront their challenges head-on, I create an environment conducive to introspection. Through probing questions and critical analysis, I encourage them to delve deep into the core of their operations, unraveling hidden potentials and latent issues. The realization derived from within often serves as a powerful catalyst for meaningful change.

Mirroring the Present:

A crucial aspect of my role is holding up a mirror to the current state of affairs. Through a candid and objective reflection of their practices, strategies, and outcomes, printers gain a clearer understanding of their strengths and weaknesses. This reflective process is not an exercise in judgment but an opportunity for constructive evaluation, paving the way for targeted improvements and strategic adjustments.

Challenging Perspectives:

In the ever-evolving landscape of the print industry, complacency is the enemy of progress. I challenge printers to question assumptions, break free from conventional molds, and explore innovative avenues. By injecting an element of healthy skepticism, I stimulate creative thinking, encouraging them to envision possibilities beyond their immediate horizons.

Data-Driven Decision Making:

Supporting my insights with concrete data and industry experience is fundamental to my consulting approach. A wealth of data exists within the industry – trends, benchmarks, success stories, and cautionary tales. By weaving this rich bundle of information into our discussions, I provide printers with a robust foundation for decision-making. Anecdotes and case studies offer valuable lessons, aiding in the formulation of informed strategies.

Encouraging Risk-Taking:

Embracing change often involves stepping into the unknown and taking calculated risks. I encourage printers to venture beyond their comfort zones, assuring them that innovation and progress often reside in uncharted territories. By fostering a culture that values calculated risk-taking, printers can position themselves as agile players in an industry that demands adaptability.

Guiding Through Challenges:

The print industry is no stranger to challenges, but each obstacle is an opportunity for growth. As a coach, my role extends beyond problem identification to strategic guidance. Together, we navigate the intricacies of specific challenges, develop contingency plans, and chart a course that aligns with both short-term goals and long-term visions.

In essence, my role is akin to a compass, helping printers navigate the intricate terrain of the industry. By instilling a sense of agency, fostering self-awareness, and providing the tools for strategic decision-making, I empower printers not only to weather industry storms but to emerge stronger and more resilient.

People Management: Nurturing Talent and Building a Vibrant Culture

People have always been the backbone of the print industry, yet talent nurturing often takes a backseat. Training, a critical element, is frequently overlooked. In my journey, I opted for a unique approach, hiring an Industrial Psychology professional on a retainer basis. This individual devised a model to assess potential hires through day-long tests, covering every aspect from technical skills to communication abilities.

Ah, the hiring conundrum—a tale of instincts, gut feelings, and the occasional curveball that comes with a promising interview pitch. Imagine this: a boardroom where potential hires showcase their finest theatrics, armed with rehearsed responses and well-practiced smiles. It's a performance that could rival Broadway, yet behind the scenes, the real show is just beginning.

In the grand theatre of recruitment, I once found myself captivated by a dazzling performance. A candidate's pitch was so convincing that I was ready to hand over the role without a second thought. Little did I know; this was a classic case of hiring blindness induced by a stellar act. The candidate, in a grand Shakespearean twist, turned out to be more Hamlet than hero.

Cue the entrance of my HR maestro, the wizard behind the hiring curtain. With a theatrical flair befitting the stage, he introduced the grand experiment—a full-day test to unravel the intricacies of a candidate's skills, character, and color perception (yes, we even checked for color blindness). The result? A performance review that ventured beyond the polished façade of an interview.

The test wasn't foolproof, of course; even the most intricate plots have their twists. Yet, it was our secret weapon, a backstage pass to uncover hidden talents and potential pitfalls. As I reflect on those days, I can't help but appreciate the irony of how a full day of scrutiny often revealed more than a carefully curated interview script.

Now, back to the theatrics. There were moments when my instincts, like an overenthusiastic understudy, urged me to skip the test and embrace the allure of gut feelings. Alas, my directorial decisions based on gut instincts resembled a Shakespearean tragedy—full of twists, turns, and often a fair share of dramatic irony.

In the end, I learned that hiring is a delicate dance between scripted performances and unscripted reality. The test days became our version of improvisational theater, where candidates couldn't rely on rehearsed lines. And as for instincts, well, let's just say they occasionally took a back seat to the unpredictable twists of the recruitment drama.

So, the next time you find yourself entranced by a stellar interview performance, remember the backstage chaos and the unscripted tests. After all, in the theater of hiring, sometimes the most dazzling acts hide the true character behind the curtain.

Managing a small team in a fledgling company is relatively straightforward, with interpersonal connections forming the fabric of the organizational culture. However, as companies grow, the challenge intensifies. Systems and processes, while essential, sometimes overshadow the softer side of employee management. To inject novelty into the routine, I introduced cross-trainings, interchangeably shifting roles within departments. This not only added a breath of fresh air but also provided employees with a sense of involvement and personal growth.

The Constant of Change:

In conclusion to this chapter - the print industry is in a perpetual state of flux. Whether in technology, people management, or customer expectations, everything evolves. The key is self-awareness – the ability to anticipate these changes. Only by acknowledging the inevitability of change can printers hope to stay ahead in this dynamic industry.

The future beckons with challenges and opportunities, but the savviest players will be those who, with foresight and adaptability, ride the waves of change rather than being swept away by them. As the curtain falls on this chapter, I urge fellow printers to embrace the winds of change, for only then can we navigate the stormy seas of the printing industry with resilience and triumph.

* *

Entrepreneur and venture capitalist Paul Graham on how to do great work:

"It's essential to work on something you're deeply interested in. Interest will drive you to work harder than mere diligence ever could. The three most powerful motives are curiosity, delight, and the desire to do something impressive. Sometimes they converge, and that combination is the most powerful of all."

Personal Reflections

In the expansive canvas of my life's journey, as I cast my gaze over, I often find myself lost in the woven threads of memories — moments of glory, ecstasy, and even moments of agony that have meticulously shaped the intricate canvas of my existence. As the retrospective architect of my own destiny, I've not merely encountered the unexpected, the unpredictable, and the unprecedented; instead, I've woven them into the very fabric of my journey. For it is in these twists and turns, traced by the brushstrokes of time, that the true beauty of the journey unfolds — a masterpiece painted with the hues of lessons learned, challenges surmounted, and triumphs celebrated.

Contrary to the conventional path trodden by business scholars, I, Warren, a maverick of sorts, never stepped into the hallowed halls of a formal business school or university. My journey, an undulating domain of challenges and triumphs, was uncharted—a thrilling odyssey propelled by an unbridled passion for the print industry that, to me, felt like home. It's not merely a profession; it's a calling, an unyielding commitment that courses through my veins, infusing life and purpose into every print endeavor.

As I stand before audiences in print forums, my passion becomes a luminous beacon, casting its warm glow on others who are yet to witness such fervor elsewhere. The stage is not just a platform; it's a sacred space where I unfold the chapters of my journey with an infectious enthusiasm that captivates, inspires, and leaves an indelible mark on the hearts of those who bear witness. The love affair with print is not a mere engagement—it's a lifelong romance that continues to evolve and deepen, forging a connection that transcends the boundaries of a conventional career. It's not about the ink and paper; it's about the essence of creation, the dance of creativity, and the symphony of stories told through the printed medium. My evolution has been a continuous learning process. I flowed with the tides, adapted to change, and embraced the multitude of lessons that each day brought. The absence of a predetermined goal or mission allowed me to meander through the complexities of entrepreneurship, making each day a canvas waiting to be painted with experiences.

Teamwork, a powerful and harmonizing mantra, became the cornerstone of my leadership philosophy as my company burgeoned. In the early days, our modus operandi was defined by study circles, a collaborative exchange of knowledge, and the nurturing of a participative work environment. However, as growth thrust us into uncharted territories, the significance of teamwork transcended mere collaboration—it became the lifeline that fueled our ascent.

In the expansive landscape of a growing enterprise, individual brilliance paled in comparison to the collective strength harnessed through collaboration. The belief in the extraordinary potential of each person gave way to the realization that true greatness lay in the synergy of minds working cohesively. No individual, regardless of their skills or talents, could singularly navigate the complexities that growth unfurled before us. The shift from personal bonding to robust systems was not a rejection of individual brilliance but an acknowledgment that, in the tapestry of our collective efforts, we could weave a narrative of unparalleled success.

As the company metamorphosed, so did my role as a leader. The dynamic interplay between personal opinions and institutional processes demanded a recalibration of my leadership style. While my initial approach involved seeking diverse opinions and implementing consensual decisions, the evolving scale necessitated a more structured adherence to established processes. The balancing act between encouraging individual voices and adhering to institutional frameworks posed a formidable challenge—one that required a nuanced understanding of when to pivot between the two paradigms. The evolution was not just a corporate transformation but a personal journey of adapting and embracing change in leadership philosophy.

Amidst the shifts, a pivotal lesson emerged—the true essence of leadership lay not in a one-size-fits-all approach but in the ability to tailor leadership strategies to the evolving needs of the organization. It was an understanding that leadership, much like the ever-changing currents of the business landscape, demanded a dynamic and adaptive mindset. The responsibility was not merely to steer the ship but to ensure that every crew member felt empowered to navigate their own course within the overarching mission.

The journey was fraught with challenges, the lessons often learned the hard way. Yet, as the company's compass pointed towards new horizons, the lessons gleaned from the crucible of growth became invaluable navigational tools. Each twist and turn served as a crucible where leadership principles were refined, tested, and emerged stronger. It was a journey of metamorphosis—a transformation from a leader shaped by circumstances to one who actively shaped the course of the company's destiny.

As the leader, the onus was not only to motivate the team but to set the tone for a culture of continuous learning. The realization dawned that leaders are not just born; they are crafted through experiences, shaped by the crucible of challenges, and honed by the fires of adversity. The journey was not just a climb up the corporate ladder; it was an exploration of uncharted territories within myself. Through the ebb and flow of the company's growth, I, too, evolved as a leader—learning, adapting, and emerging resilient in the face of evolving challenges.

In the realm of leadership, I discovered the delicate dance between holding the reins firmly and allowing the team the autonomy to navigate their roles. The leadership journey was not about wielding authority but about creating an environment where every team member felt not just a sense of belonging but also a sense of ownership. It was about fostering a culture where everyone contributed to the symphony of success, each note resonating with the collective vision.

In the symphony of growth, the conductor, once the sole orchestrator of decisions, evolved into a collaborative leader. The transition from a directive approach to one that embraced the wisdom of the collective marked a turning point. It was a realization that the most impactful decisions were often forged through the crucible of collective insights, diverse perspectives, and the amalgamation of individual strengths. The power of teamwork was not just a corporate cliche; it was the bedrock upon which the edifice of our success was erected.

As the tapestry of the company's journey unfolded, every thread represented not just the individual contributions of team members but the interwoven fabric of shared victories and collective accomplishments. The symphony of teamwork, composed of diverse instruments playing in harmony, resonated through the corridors of our corporate existence. It was an acknowledgment that the true magic happened not in the solitary brilliance of individual notes but in the seamless blend of each instrument, creating a harmonious melody that echoed the spirit of our collective aspirations.

The ethos of participative decision-making was not a departure from individual brilliance but an elevation of it. It was an acknowledgment that no single person, regardless of their prowess, could anticipate the multifaceted challenges that growth presented. The journey from personal bonding to robust systems was not a relinquishment of individual brilliance but a realization that true greatness lay in the synergy of minds working cohesively. In the grand tapestry of corporate evolution, teamwork emerged as the dynamic thread that wove together the intricate patterns of success.

In the labyrinth of growth, the belief that any one individual possessed the omniscience to navigate the complexities gave way to an understanding—the true genius lay in the collective wisdom of the team.

Leadership, a mantle I donned with a profound sense of responsibility, transcended the conventional contours of authority. The essence of leadership wasn't confined to being a boss; it became an intrinsic facet of my identity. It demanded a multifaceted approach, embracing ethics, meritocracy, and unwavering resolve. The weight of decisions rested squarely on my shoulders, and in navigating the complexities, leadership emerged not merely as a role but as a testament to character.

A leader, I discovered, was not just a motivator but a beacon—illuminating the path others chose to follow. The role extended beyond steering the ship; it was about fostering an environment where every team member felt empowered, heard, and integral to the collective journey. Leadership, in its quintessence, was a manifestation of character—a reflection of fairness, a commitment to meritocracy, and an embodiment of the values that defined our corporate identity.

In the grand tapestry of leadership, the true measure was not the authority one wielded but the impact one left on the ethos of the organization. It was about fostering a culture where leadership was a collective endeavor—a collaborative symphony where each team member played a unique note, contributing to the harmonious melody of success. Leadership wasn't a solo performance; it was an ensemble cast, each playing a pivotal role in shaping the narrative of achievement.

The journey illuminated the fact that true leadership was an amalgamation of diverse qualities—decisiveness in moments of uncertainty, empathy in understanding the team's needs, and resilience in the face of challenges. It was about setting a tone of accountability, where leaders didn't merely dictate but actively participated in the collective pursuit of excellence. The metamorphosis from being a boss to becoming a leader was not a relinquishing of authority; it was an evolution into a more profound understanding of the role's transformative potential.

Leadership was not a title bestowed but a continuous journey of personal and professional growth. It was about navigating the delicate balance between authority and empathy, forging a connection with the team that transcended hierarchical boundaries. A leader was not just a decision-maker; they were a catalyst for change, an advocate for growth, and a guardian of the organizational ethos. The true test of leadership lay not in moments of triumph but in the resilience displayed during adversities.

As I reflect on this leadership journey, it becomes apparent that leadership wasn't a destination but an ongoing exploration. It was a dynamic interplay of skills, adaptability, and a deep-seated commitment to the well-being of the team. Every decision, every course correction, and every moment of inspiration were threads woven into the fabric of leadership—a fabric that bore the imprints of shared victories, collective resilience, and a commitment to fostering a culture of excellence.

The journey of leadership was a testament to the belief that leaders are not just born; they are sculpted through experiences, shaped by challenges, and refined through the crucible of evolving responsibilities. It was an acknowledgment that the true measure of leadership was not in the title one held but in the impact one left on the hearts and minds of the team. As the leader, I didn't just dictate the course; I became a part of the narrative, contributing my thread to the rich tapestry of our collective journey.

In conclusion, leadership wasn't a badge worn for recognition; it was a responsibility shouldered for the greater good. It was the ability to inspire, the commitment to values, and the relentless pursuit of a shared vision. The journey of leadership was not a solitary walk but a collective march, where every team member played a crucial role in shaping the trajectory of success. As I look back on this transformative expedition, I recognize that the true essence of leadership lies not in the destination but in the perpetual pursuit of becoming better versions of ourselves.

Dyslexia may have curtailed my voracious reading habits, but two books, like lighthouses in the vast sea of literature, guided my ship. "Fish: A Proven Way to Boost Morale and Improve Results" by by Stephen C. Lundin (Author), Harry Paul (Author), John Christensen (Author), Ken Blanchard (Foreword), taught me practical lessons in customer service, trust-building, teamwork, and leadership. "Who Moved My Cheese" by Dr. Spencer Johnson became a mastery guide, leaving an indelible mark on my approach to change and adaptation.

Here are my key takeaways:

"Fish: A Proven Way to Boost Morale and Improve Results" by by Stephen C. Lundin (Author), Harry Paul (Author), John Christensen (Author), Ken Blanchard (Foreword)

1. **Practical Lessons for Customer Service:** The book offers actionable insights into enhancing customer service, emphasizing the importance of creating positive interactions and memorable experiences.

2. **Building Trust:** "Fish" underscores the significance of trust in a workplace. It provides strategies to build and maintain trust among team members, fostering a cohesive and supportive environment.

3. **Teamwork:** A central theme is the promotion of teamwork. The book provides real-world examples and techniques to encourage collaboration, shared goals, and a sense of camaraderie among team members.

4. **Leadership Boost:** Practical leadership lessons are woven into the narrative. It explores how effective leadership contributes to improved morale and results, offering guidance on inspiring and guiding teams.

"Who Moved My Cheese" by Dr. Spencer Johnson

1. **Adaptation to Change:** The book serves as a mastery guide for navigating change. It imparts valuable lessons on adapting to unexpected shifts, both in professional and personal spheres.

2. **Anticipation and Proactivity:** "Who Moved My Cheese" encourages readers to anticipate change and proactively seek new opportunities. It emphasizes the importance of staying ahead in dynamic environments.

3. **Resilience and Flexibility:** The narrative highlights the resilience and flexibility needed to thrive in ever-evolving circumstances. It instills a mindset that views change not as a threat but as a gateway to growth.

4. **Personal and Professional Adaptability:** Dr. Spencer Johnson's work provides insights into the seamless integration of personal and professional adaptability. It inspires individuals to embrace change as a constant in their journey.

These takeaways encapsulate the essence of the books, offering readers practical wisdom and a mindset shift towards positive change, effective leadership, and a collaborative work environment.

THE PRINTING INDUSTRY AUTHORITY

graphic

MONTHLY CANADA

OCTOBER 08
VOL.29 NO.5
$7.00

PERFECT
BINDING
OPTIONS
FOR SHORT
RUNS

FINISHES
THAT
MAKE A
SPLASH

Warren Werbitt,
president,
Pazazz Printing

Warren Werbitt
PRINTER OF THE YEAR

Printer of the Year 2008

Throughout my journey, two influential figures altered the trajectory of my thoughts and business practices. Remi Marcoux of Transcontinental Inc., a giant in the printing industry, shared the spotlight with me as we were both honoured as Canadian printers of the year but I was the first one in the rank. Brian O'Keefe of O'keefe Printing left an indelible mark on me with his commitment to quality, innovative practices, and unparalleled customer value.

In the grand theatre of my life, personal milestones rose to the spotlight with the arrival of my two little showstoppers. Professionally, the unexpected narrative unfolded like a blockbuster, starring me as the boss, seated in a throne-like chair, directing a team, and steering the company through the turbulent waves of growth—an unimaginable blockbuster beyond the wildest scenes I had envisioned. The script took unpredictable turns, from gracing the sacred grounds of Drupa to unveiling the "Printings Alive" video, earning applause, and orchestrating a jaw-dropping USD 7 million investment budget in the stormy seas of 2008.

Navigating the swirling currents, confronting challenges that popped up like surprise plot twists, each step not only revealed the destination but also the sheer joy bubbling in every stride. The unpredictable journey wasn't just a ride; it was a rollercoaster of emotions, a comedy of errors, and a drama of resilience—an epic saga worthy of the silver screen.

Friends meeting up in Drupa 2024

Print Reimagined:
A Maverick's Odyssey Through Past, Present, and Future

As I reflect on these years, there's an overwhelming sense of wonder and gratitude. I haven't just embraced print; I've submerged myself in its essence, and we've become inseparable. Print has been my guide, opening my eyes, nurturing my curiosity, and unveiling the authentic me. Much like print, I speak from the heart, unfiltered and genuine.

The allure of print lies in its ability to transform concepts into tangible realities—a dream materializing before our eyes.

Immersed in a world of colours, expressions, and fantasies, print has the remarkable power to bring imagination to life.

Print isn't a mere medium; it's a silent storyteller woven into the fabric of everyday life. It touches every facet, leaving its mark everywhere you turn. Throughout my journey in the print realm, I've been fortunate to cross paths with extraordinary individuals. Witnessing their growth and evolution has, in turn, broadened my perspective and enriched my experience.

Throughout the years, I've transformed into a spokesperson for the print industry, a role where my opinions (sometimes) hold weight and significance. Witnessing printers, executives, OEMs, and trade bodies patiently listen and incorporate my views into their plans has been immensely gratifying. There have been numerous proud moments, instances where the impact of my passion, commitment, and the value I bring to the table became evident. It's heartening to see how my voice has resonated within the industry, influencing decisions and contributing to the collective progress of the print community.

Who on earth says print is on life support? The perpetual debate about the death or survival of print never ceases to amuse me. Let's get real, folks—print is not bowing out; it's gearing up for a dazzling makeover. With the unstoppable march of technology, print is set to morph into a multimedia marvel. It's not about print OR digital; it's about a vibrant coexistence. No sane marketer will bid adieu to print entirely; they'll just have to orchestrate a symphony with all the media maestros at their disposal.

Look at this: a fusion of colors and intricate detailing propelling print into the world of hyper-reality. Technology, with its wizardry of improved machines, AI, and machine learning, will be the trusty steed riding print into the future. Self-publishing has turned the dream of becoming an author into a cakewalk. Print on Demand has made reaching the last mile a stroll in the park. Local printers are high-fiving each other as they team up for those last-mile deliveries.

Print is not in a rivalry; it's the ultimate collaborator. I bought a pair of shoes the other day, and the packaging was like a fashion show, with five different labels sashaying around besides the main carton. So, is print waving its final goodbye? Nah, look at the evolution of direct mailers and marketing. It's all about personalized and customized offers—a game everyone wants to play. Focused marketing is the secret sauce for results and conversions, and print is the Most Valued Proposition contributing to the victory. Let's face it, folks, print is not dying; it's getting a front-row seat to the tech-fueled spectacle of its own renaissance!

If I were in the market for a superstar salesman today, I wouldn't settle for anything less than the Michael Jordan of client relations. Here's my blueprint for the ideal candidate who'd not just knock on doors but blow them wide open:

1. **Presentation and Communication Mastery:** I need someone who can make our pitch sound like a symphony, a performance that leaves clients nodding in agreement, not scratching their heads.

2. **Open-ended Attitude and a Hunger for Learning:** I want someone with an insatiable appetite for knowledge, a hunger to learn, and an attitude that says, "Challenge accepted!"

3. **Listening Skills on Steroids:** Give me a sales therapist. Someone who doesn't just hear but listens, decoding the client's needs like Sherlock Holmes solves a case. The person should be able to hear what the customer didn't say.

4. **Team Player Extraordinaire:** We're not playing the solo game; we're in a relay race. I want a team player who understands that the victory lies in passing the baton seamlessly through the entire process of customer acquisition.

5. **Empathy as the Secret Sauce:** Empathy isn't just a skill; it's the magic wand that turns potential clients into

loyal advocates. Our sales magician needs to wield it with finesse.

6. **Understanding the Customer's Customer:** I want someone who can go beyond the surface, diving deep into understanding not just our client but their clientele too.

7. **Tech-Savvy Instincts:** In a world where tech is king, my ideal candidate should be the Jedi of the digital canvas —navigating with finesse, and wielding gadgets like lightsabers.

So, if you think you're not just a salesman but a sales wizard ready to weave magic, I would welcome you to the team!

Let me paint you a vivid picture of the printer's struggle: there I am, the eager buyer, my pockets loaded with half a million dollars, excitedly gazing at this gleaming piece of machinery— the Apple of all printers, the Ferrari of the press world. The salesman, equally thrilled about his commission, passionately extols the virtues of this printing behemoth, promising me a utopia of efficiency and productivity.

Fast forward a few weeks, and the honeymoon phase with my new printing marvel comes to a grinding halt. The machine throws a tantrum, refusing to cooperate. Panic sets in;

production grinds to a halt, and I'm left watching my money go down the drain with every passing idle moment.

The cavalry arrives in the form of the company's support team, armed with apologies, promises, and assurances. But hold on a minute—what about my bank instalments? They don't hit pause because my printer is taking an unscheduled siesta. The company that sold me the machine? They're oblivious to my financial woes and certainly don't offer a grace period in the instalment timeline **– that's knowing your customer.**

Who also bears the brunt of this downtime? Yours truly, my eventual buyer. It's not just a delay in production; it's a ripple effect—my customers face delays, product launches get shoved, deadlines are missed, and the brand takes a hit. Yet, in the grand scheme of things, I'm the one left juggling the financial and reputational repercussions **– that's knowing your customer's customer.**

Now, let's talk about the seemingly innocuous application form. Imagine this: a cramped space, barely enough room to squeeze in my name and email address. It's a puzzle, and the pieces don't fit. Does the salesman ever take a moment to point this out? Rarely.

Imagine a world where the salesman becomes the unsung hero, the advocate for spacious application forms. Picture a scenario where they say, "Hey, your details deserve space to breathe, room to be noticed. Let's not cramp your style." It's not just about printing; it's about creating an experience, adding value, and standing out from the crowd.

So, printers of the world, think beyond the ink. Consider these nuances, the unsaid pain points of your clients, and turn them into moments where you shine. Differentiation lies not just in what you print but how you understand, empathize, and elevate the entire experience for your clients. It's not just printing; it's a performance, a masterpiece on the canvas of customer satisfaction.

Ah, the glorious days of yore when we ventured into the print business with an air of nonchalance, expecting customers to flock to us like moths to a flame. Machines were bought with a casual "everything for everyone" mindset. Build it, and they will come, right? Little did we know, or care to think.

Fast forward to today, and the stark reality hits like a ton of bricks. If I were to embark on this journey anew, 'preparation' would be my mantra, echoing through every decision like a well-rehearsed symphony.

Imagine the stage being set, the curtains slowly parting to reveal a meticulously crafted 'Business Plan' stealing the spotlight. The audience, a congregation of potential clients, spellbound by a 'Marketing Plan' that doesn't just whisper but shouts, "We are here, and we mean business!"

The cast, my dedicated team, carefully selected through a rigorous hiring process, each member a crucial note in the melody of success. Data, the unsung hero, takes center stage. In the immortal words of W. Edwards Deming, "In God we trust; all others must bring data." The script demands it, and every decision bows before the might of data.

Funding and investment discussions unfold like a Shakespearean drama, with ROI playing the protagonist. Segments and regions are strategically chosen, a chessboard of potential conquests. Forecasts and measurements cast a crystal ball's gaze into the future, steering us toward prosperity.

Ah, the future—a stage where machines hum in harmony with AI, collaborating seamlessly. Niche building and specialization become our artistic signature, the brushstrokes of a masterpiece in the making.

But let's not forget marketing—the dazzling showstopper. No longer can we rely on the whispers of word-of-mouth alone.

Social media, the Internet, technological acrobatics, direct marketing, sampling, and prototyping—they all join the cast. Webinars become our educational sonnets, and networking our grand ballroom dance.

And amid this symphony of preparedness, one resounding truth echoes: print is here to stay. The question, my friends, is not whether print will endure but whether you are prepared to dance to its evolving rhythm. Adapt, evolve, and let the drama unfold!

Key Takeaways

In the final chapter of this captivating journey through the vibrant canvas of the print industry, let's pause for reflection. As we delve into the nuances of both personal and professional worlds, the amalgamation of these narratives offers readers a unique prism through which to view the remarkable evolution of an indus try and an individual. Our expedition has traversed technological revolutions, entrepreneurial challenges, and the indomitable spirit that propels one forward in the pursuit of passion. Now, in this concluding chapter, let's distill the essence of this odyssey, summarizing the key takeaways that will linger in the minds of readers – lessons forged in the crucible of experience, moments of triumph, and the unrelenting pursuit of excellence.

1. **Passion for Print:** Discovering one's passion is like finding the compass that guides a ship through uncharted waters. For me, that guiding force has been an unbridled passion for the enchanting world of print. As we navigate through the chapters of my journey, I urge you to embark on a quest to uncover your own passion, the driving force that propels you toward excellence. Let the vibrant hues of print and the tales they carry inspire you to seek and embrace what sets your soul ablaze. Here's what Steve Jobs said about following one's dreams is encapsulated in the following quote: "Your work is going to fill a large part of your life, and the only way to be truly satisfied is to do what you believe is great work. And the only way to do great work is to love what you do. If you haven't found it yet, keep looking. Don't settle. As with all matters of the heart, you'll know when you find it." For me this is passion.

2. **Adaptability:** In the ever-changing landscape of the print industry, I've learned that adaptability is not just a choice but a necessity.

3. **Evolution of Technology:** From the era of Desktop Publishing to the current age of AI and automation, witness in the earlier pages the remarkable technological evolution within the print industry.

4. **Variable Data Printing (VDP):** Discover how personalization through Variable Data Printing has transformed marketing, forging a tangible connection with customers.

5. **Print on Demand (POD):** Picture a landscape where aspiring authors hold the reins, where the traditional barriers of printing logistics crumble, and where creativity finds its canvas without constraints. Print on Demand, the revolutionary heartbeat of this transformation, is set to redefine the self-publishing narrative. No longer bound by the limitations of large print runs or extensive pre-investment, authors can now bring their literary creations to life seamlessly, one copy at a time. This paradigm shift is not just a mere evolution; it's a revolution in the making. As the self-publishing industry continues to thrive, POD emerges as the game-changer, offering authors the agility to respond to market demands swiftly. With the ability to print on a per-order basis, authors no longer need to navigate the complexities of predicting demand or managing excessive inventory. The power to publish becomes a democratic tool, placing the author in the driver's seat, steering the course of their literary destiny. Moreover, the democratization of distribution channels becomes palpable with POD, ensuring that every aspiring author has an equal shot at reaching a

global audience. Traditional publishing gatekeepers fade into the background, making way for a more inclusive literary landscape where talent takes precedence over preconceived notions. Imagine a world where creativity knows no bounds, where authors can experiment with diverse genres, themes, and formats without the constraints of commercial viability. Print on Demand opens the door to this world, fostering an environment where authors can explore the depths of their imagination and bring forth literary works that resonate authentically with their vision. In the realm of self-publishing, the future is Print on Demand — a future where the power of storytelling rests firmly in the hands of those who craft the narratives. Join me in envisioning this transformative journey where Print on Demand becomes the catalyst for a new era in self-publishing, breaking barriers, and unleashing the full potential of literary expression.

6. **Smart Packaging:** Uncover the integration of smart packaging technologies, adding interactivity and traceability to products on the shelves. Keep observing the number of printed items you get every time you order something online or buy from the stores. Print is everywhere.

7. **AI and Automation Integration:** Artificial intelligence and automation play pivotal roles in predictive maintenance, quality control, and process optimization.

8. **Augmented Reality (AR) in Print:** Embrace these future technologies. This space will get more exciting ahead.

9. **Lessons in Pricing:** I shared insights on getting pricing right, covering costs, and ensuring profitability in a fiercely competitive market. Get efficiency in your print operations.

10. **Quality Matters:** Understand why maintaining high-quality standards is non-negotiable and how defining "good" is a key consideration.

11. **Good Practices:** Your journey from good to great is in your hands. Embracing the philosophy of continuous improvement and adherence to good practices for overall success is what I've highlighted.

12. **Environmental Responsibility:** Adapting to eco-friendly practices and contributing to the global environmental movement is a measured activity you will have to undertake.

13. **Operational Efficiency:** The heart of profitability lies in operational efficiency. Work on optimizing processes and workflows for success.

14. **Effective Production Scheduling:** Learn the art of scheduling effectively, leaving room for surprises, and managing client expectations for successful production.

15. **Common Sense in Business:** In our business journey, I emphasized seeking help when needed, asking questions, and applying common sense in decision-making.

16. **Teamwork:** Understand the pivotal role of teamwork, with insights into managing small teams, fostering a positive work culture, and introducing cross-training.

17. **Leadership Skills:** Leadership isn't just a role; it's an intrinsic quality. Explore with me the ethical, meritocratic, and motivating aspects of leadership.

18. **Talent Nurturing:** I shed light on the historical oversight in nurturing talent within our industry and propose innovative hiring practices.

19. **Learning from Mistakes:** Embrace the wisdom that lies in learning from pricing mistakes, welcoming failures, and the ongoing journey of continuous improvement.

20. **Customer-Centric Approach:** Join me in recognizing printers as brand custodians, emphasizing the need for a customer-centric approach in every facet of our work.

21. **Competitor Analysis:** Uncover my creative approach of hiring a lady to gather insights from competitors, showcasing innovative thinking in understanding market dynamics.

22. **Continuous Learning:** Embrace the importance of being a perpetual learner, adapting to changes, and staying curious – keys to our enduring growth.

23. **Print's Enduring Relevance:** In the midst of debates on the fate of print, envision with me a future where print coexists harmoniously with other media, driven by technological fusion and consumer preferences.

Epilogue

As we reach the end of this journey through the vibrant world of printing, it's time to take a moment to reflect and look ahead. This book has been a labour of love, filled with the highs and lows, as well as the victories and setbacks that have defined my career in the print industry.

Throughout these pages, we've explored the essence of print – its challenges, its beauty, and its ever-evolving nature. From the early days of setting up Pazazz Printing to navigating the stormy seas of economic downturns and technological advancements, this journey has been nothing short of extraordinary. The stories shared here are more than just anecdotes; they are lessons learned, insights gained, and a testament to the resilience and creativity that the print industry demands.

Reflecting on the Journey:

Writing this book has been a reflective process, taking me back through the pivotal moments that shaped not only my business but also my personal growth. The long hours, the relentless pursuit of excellence, and the unwavering belief in the power of print have all been part of this incredible journey. It's been a path filled with innovation, a bit of madness, and a ton of passion. The challenges we faced, from the intricacies of die-cutting Christmas cards to the ambitious endeavor of printing on plastic, tested our limits and pushed us to innovate and adapt.

Providing Additional Insights:

Since completing the main chapters of this book, the print industry continues to evolve at a rapid pace. New digital printing technologies, AI-enhanced software and solutions, and the data! Don't get me started on the data. These are all transforming how we think about print and its applications. Sustainability is no longer just a buzzword but a critical component of every print operation. The integration of digital tools and automation is streamlining workflows and enhancing efficiency. Staying ahead of these trends is crucial for anyone in this industry, and I am excited to see how these advancements will continue to shape our future.

Sharing Reader Engagement:

The feedback and reactions from early readers have been immensely encouraging. Many have reached out to share how the book has inspired them, provided them with new insights, or simply made them laugh with its candid tales. These connections reinforce the idea that we are all part of a larger community, bound by our shared passion for print. The real-world impact of this book is a reminder of why we do what we do – to inspire, to innovate, and to leave a lasting impression.

Looking ahead, I am thrilled about the projects on the horizon. The Print Whisperer is more than just a consultancy; it's a mission to help other print businesses thrive. The lessons I've learned and the experiences I've gathered are tools I now use to guide others. There are new areas to explore, new challenges to overcome, and new stories to create. The future of print is bright, and I am eager to be part of it.

Expressing Gratitude:

I owe a debt of gratitude to so many people who have been part of this journey. To my family, whose support has been unwavering, to my colleagues and employees who have stood by me through thick and thin, and to the mentors who have guided me along the way – thank you. Your contributions have been invaluable, and this book is as much yours as it is mine.

Ending with a Strong Message:

Closing this chapter, I leave you with a thought: in an age where everything is rapidly digitizing, print remains a tangible, powerful medium. It's more than just ink (or toner, or inkjet) on paper; it's a craft, an art, and a testament to human ingenuity. Embrace the challenges, innovate with passion, and always remember that the printed word holds a unique power – a power to inform, to inspire, and to endure.

As we reach the final impression of this book, I hope you've enjoyed this print-run through my colourful journey. Like the perfect ink density that convert stunning visuals to everlasting stories, I've tried to share my experiences with clarity and vivid detail. Remember, life's too short to worry about the gutter margins—embrace the chaos and find your unique binding style with customers, vendors, employees and even competition.

Whether your days feel embossed with triumphs or debossed with challenges, know that the right grammage of experience and the perfect engagement can make all the difference.

Thank you for flipping through these pages and becoming part of my story. If you've got any thoughts, questions, or just want to share your own print escapades, don't hesitate to drop me an email. After all, the best stories are those that are shared, reprinted, and passed along.

Non-Ink stained regards,

Warren Werbitt

warren@theprintwhisperer.com

References:

- Ikigai - https://en.wikipedia.org/wiki/Ikigai

- Steve Jobs quotes: https://blog.hubspot.com/sales/steve-jobs-quotes

- www.hardingpoorman.com

- https://jamesclear.com/

- Fish: A Proven Way to Boost Morale and Improve Results Hardcover – by Stephen C. Lundin (Author), Harry Paul (Author), John Christensen (Author), Ken Blanchard (Foreword): https://a.co/d/0YPhiVm

- Who Moved My Cheese by Dr Spencer Johnson: https://amzn.eu/d/jdrFlAr